PAT BROWN, MBA

DanceMoney101

Using Dance to Teach the Basics of Money

ABRAM 47 BROWN

First published by AbramBrown47 2026

First edition

ISBN: 978-1-967737-59-8

This book was professionally typeset on Reedsy.
Find out more at reedsy.com

Contents

Foreword

Dance teaches you discipline long before it teaches you applause.

Long before the lights come up, before the music starts, before anyone is watching, dancers learn how to show up. You learn how to repeat the same movement until it is clean. You learn how to hold balance under pressure. You learn how to accept correction without taking it personally. You learn that progress is rarely linear and that mastery takes time.

Those lessons matter far beyond the studio.

What dance does *not* teach very well is how to manage money once the performance ends.

Many dancers spend years in environments where the schedule is set, the next rehearsal is known, and the focus is entirely on the craft. Income, when it comes, is often irregular. Some seasons are full. Others are quiet. Paychecks may come from multiple sources: contracts, gigs, teaching, performances, appearances, or side work that keeps everything moving. There is rarely one clean path, and there is almost never a standard playbook.

That is not a failure of dancers. It is a gap in education.

This book exists to close that gap.

Dance Money 101 is not about turning dancers into accountants or asking artists to abandon creativity. It is about giving performers the same structure for money that they already understand in training. Just as technique protects your body, financial fundamentals protect your future. Just as balance and control matter more than flash, consistency and discipline matter more than big financial wins.

The truth is simple and often uncomfortable: talent alone does not sustain a career. Neither does passion. Longevity comes from preparation, smart decisions, and systems that hold up when circumstances change. Money is one of those systems, whether dancers like it or not.

This book respects the reality of dance careers. It recognizes that:

- Income is rarely predictable
- Careers evolve over time
- Bodies need recovery
- Opportunities come in waves
- Identity can feel fragile when the stage goes quiet

Rather than offering shortcuts or hype, this book focuses on fundamentals. Saving. Budgeting. Risk awareness. Investing with patience. Protecting yourself from mistakes that quietly derail careers. These are not glamorous topics, but neither are pliés, tendus, or conditioning drills. They are foundational, and they work.

Most importantly, this book treats dancers as whole people.

Not just performers.

Not just athletes.

Not just artists.

But individuals with long lives, changing priorities, families, responsibilities, and futures that extend well beyond any single role or stage.

The goal of **Dance Money 101** is not to help you "get rich." The goal is to help you stay balanced, make informed decisions, and build stability so that money supports your career instead of controlling it. Financial confidence creates creative freedom. When money is handled intentionally, dancers can take opportunities because they want to, not because they are forced to.

If you have ever felt overwhelmed by money, behind compared to others, or unsure how long you can keep doing what you love, you are not alone. This book was written for you.

The performance may end.

But the career, the life, and the person behind the movement deserve to continue with strength, balance, and purpose.

Introduction

Every dancer knows the moment.

The music fades. The lights dim. The applause rises, then disappears. You bow, exit the stage, and the adrenaline slowly drains away. For a few minutes, everything you trained for feels complete.

And then reality returns.

Dance careers are built on moments, but life is built in the space between them. Rehearsals end. Contracts expire. Seasons change. Bodies recover. Roles evolve. What often catches dancers off guard is not the work itself, but what comes after the work stops for the day, the month, or the year.

The performance ends, but the career continues.

Money shows up most clearly in those in-between moments.

Unlike traditional careers with predictable salaries and benefits, dance income is often irregular. Some months are full. Others are quiet. You might juggle performances, teaching, freelance work, appearances, choreography, or side jobs that make the schedule possible. That variability is normal in dance, but it requires a different kind of preparation.

Most dancers are trained to manage their bodies under pressure, but not their finances.

You learn how to rehearse through fatigue.

You learn how to take notes without ego.

You learn how to push through discomfort and stay disciplined.

You learn how to keep going even when the outcome is uncertain.

Those skills matter with money too, even if no one ever explained that connection.

Many dancers assume financial stability is something you figure out later. After the big break. After the next contract. After things settle down. The problem is that "later" often arrives without warning. An injury. A canceled tour. A role that does not renew. A shift in priorities. When money has never been part of the system, those transitions feel heavier than they need to be.

This book exists because dancers deserve better preparation.

Not hype.

Not fear.

Not unrealistic promises.

Just fundamentals.

Dance already teaches you the mindset required for financial success. Balance. Precision. Repetition. Patience. Awareness. The challenge is learning how to apply those same principles outside the studio.

Money, like dance, is not about perfection. You can hit every step and still lose balance at the end. You can earn well and still struggle if decisions are rushed or reactive. What matters is control, consistency, and the ability to adjust without panicking.

That is what this book focuses on.

You will not find shortcuts here.

You will not find get-rich-quick stories.

You will not be told to abandon creativity for spreadsheets.

Instead, you will learn how to:

- Build stability around unpredictable income
- Make decisions without emotional whiplash
- Protect yourself from common mistakes performers make
- Use money as a support system, not a source of stress

This is not about leaving dance behind. It is about making sure dance does not leave you behind.

The best performers think beyond the next eight counts. They think about longevity, sustainability, and recovery. Financial decisions deserve the same respect. When money is handled intentionally, it gives you options. Options allow you to choose opportunities based on growth, not desperation.

The curtain may close on a performance.

But the career, the life, and the person behind the movement continue long after the music stops.

This book is your guide for that part of the journey.

About This Book

Dance is built on discipline, repetition, and control. Money works the same way, even though it is rarely taught that way to dancers.

From the outside, dance can look expressive and free. From the inside, you know the truth. Every performance rests on fundamentals that are practiced daily. Balance is trained, not hoped for. Timing is earned through repetition. Technique protects you when pressure rises. When something goes wrong mid-performance, you adjust without stopping the show.

Financial decisions follow the same rules.

This book is not about turning dancers into finance professionals. It is about translating skills you already have into an area of life that quietly determines your freedom, stress level, and long-term options.

Dance teaches you to respect process over outcome. You do not master a turn by forcing it once. You master it through consistent reps, honest feedback, and patience. Money rewards the same behavior. Small, steady decisions made over time matter more than dramatic moves made under pressure.

Dance also teaches you that careers are rarely linear. Some seasons are full of opportunity. Others are about rebuilding, healing, or waiting. Income often reflects that rhythm. Financial systems must be built to support irregular schedules, freelance work, contracts, and transitions, not fight against them.

Many dancers struggle with money not because they lack discipline, but because no one showed them how to apply it financially. Saving can feel restrictive. Investing can feel intimidating. Planning can feel overwhelming when income is unpredictable. This book reframes those ideas using language dancers already understand.

Budgeting becomes balance.

Saving becomes injury protection.

Investing becomes long-term conditioning.

Risk becomes choreography choice.

Consistency becomes career longevity.

Throughout this book, dance is not a metaphor added for decoration. It is the framework. Each financial concept is explained through movement, rehearsal, performance cycles, and career realities dancers actually face. Whether your background is ballet, hip hop, competitive dance, cheer dance, cultural dance, ballroom, or commercial work, the principles hold.

This book also respects the emotional side of dance. Perfectionism, comparison, pressure, and identity are part of the culture. Those same forces show up in financial decisions. Overspending to keep up. Avoiding money because it feels uncomfortable. Taking unnecessary risks out of fear of missing out. These patterns are not personal flaws. They are predictable responses to uncertainty.

Just like technique improves with awareness, financial habits improve once you can see what is happening clearly.

You will not be asked to abandon creativity or spontaneity. You will be asked to build a structure that supports them. When money is handled intentionally, it becomes quieter. It stops competing for attention. That is when you can focus more fully on your craft, your health, and your future.

Dance careers do not last forever in the same form. Bodies change. Priorities evolve. Opportunities shift. What endures is the discipline dancers carry with them. This book is designed to make sure that discipline translates into stability, confidence, and choice long after the performance ends.

Dance already taught you how to do hard things over time.

This book shows you how to let those lessons work for your money too.

Foolish Assumptions

Every book makes assumptions. Some are wrong. Some are incomplete. This section is upfront about what this book assumes about you, not to judge you, but to set expectations clearly.

First, this book assumes you are disciplined, even if you do not always feel disciplined with money.

If you train, rehearse, perform, or teach dance in any form, you already understand structure. You show up when you are tired. You repeat movements that are uncomfortable. You accept correction. You commit to long timelines with no guaranteed payoff. Those behaviors are discipline. If they do not always show up in your finances, it is not because you lack them. It is because no one taught you how to apply them there.

Second, this book assumes you care deeply about your craft, sometimes at the expense of your own stability.

Many dancers were taught, directly or indirectly, that focusing on money somehow cheapens the art. That survival should come second to passion. That sacrifice is proof of commitment. This book assumes you have felt that tension. It also assumes you are ready to challenge the idea that struggle is required for authenticity.

Caring about money does not mean you care less about dance. It means you want the ability to continue choosing dance without constant stress.

Third, this book assumes your income has not followed a clean, predictable path.

Whether you perform, compete, teach, choreograph, freelance, or juggle multiple roles, your earnings likely fluctuate. Some months feel abundant. Others feel thin. Traditional financial advice often assumes a steady paycheck and ignores this reality. This book assumes your financial system needs flexibility, not rigidity, and that planning is more important for variable income, not less.

Fourth, this book assumes you have made financial decisions based on emotion at some point.

That might look like spending after a big performance. Avoiding bills because they trigger anxiety. Saying yes to work that paid poorly out of fear of missing opportunity. Or taking financial risks without fully understanding them. These are not failures. They are human responses to uncertainty, pressure, and identity. This book assumes you want to make decisions with more clarity going forward.

Fifth, this book assumes you do not need to be perfect to improve.

Dance culture often rewards perfectionism. Money punishes it. Waiting to start until everything is ideal usually leads to inaction. This book assumes you are willing to work with imperfect information, make small adjustments, and improve over time. Progress matters more than flawless execution.

Sixth, this book assumes you want options later, even if you are focused on the present.

You may love where you are right now. You may also know that bodies change, priorities shift, and careers evolve. This book assumes you want future flexibility. Not because you are planning to leave dance, but because you respect yourself enough to prepare for what comes next.

Finally, this book assumes you are capable of learning this.

You do not need a finance background. You do not need to enjoy spreadsheets. You do not need to change who you are. You only need the same mindset you already bring into the studio: willingness to learn, patience with the process, and commitment to the work.

If any of these assumptions feel uncomfortable, that is okay. Growth often starts there.

About Pat Brown

Pat Brown played college football at the University of Kansas from 1994 to 1999 and was named team captain for the 1999 season. His years in the locker room shaped his views on accountability, discipline, preparation, and leadership—principles that continue to guide his work long after football.

Following his playing career, Pat transitioned into financial services and built a career as a financial advisor and wealth manager. He works with individuals, families, business owners, and athletes navigating increasingly complex financial lives. He pursued advanced education and professional development, earning an MBA along with industry designations including ChFC®, RICP®, and CAP®. His background blends academic training with real-world experience in financial planning, retirement income strategies, tax planning, and philanthropy.

As the college sports landscape evolved, Pat recognized a persistent education gap facing athletes. Dancers, like many athletes, dedicate years to discipline, repetition, performance, and precision, yet often receive little to no guidance on managing income, budgeting irregular pay, planning for transitions, or building long-term financial stability. That disconnect between effort and financial understanding became a driving force behind his work.

Pat has since become a recognized voice in athlete financial education and has been interviewed by national publications and platforms including *Financial Planning, Yahoo,* and *ESPN Andscape,* where he shares insights on financial literacy gaps, athlete income volatility, and the challenges performers face during and after their competitive years.

These experiences led Pat to author a series of practical, athlete-focused books designed to meet athletes and families where they are. His NIL-related titles include *Financial Literacy for NIL, Financial Literacy for NIL for Parents of Student Athletes, Financial Literacy for NIL for High School Students,* and *Financial Literacy for NIL for International Student Athletes.* Each book is written to be clear, accessible, and grounded in real-world scenarios rather than theory.

Pat also created a growing collection of sport- and performance-specific financial education titles, including *Football Money 101, Baseball Money 101, Basketball Money 101, Cheer Money 101, Dance Money 101, Gymnastics Money 101, Hockey Money 101, Lacrosse Money 101, Rowing Money 101, Soccer Money 101, Softball Money 101, Tennis Money 101, Track Money 101, Volleyball Money 101,* and *Wrestling Money 101.* Each book translates the culture, discipline, structure, and mental demands of the activity into financial lessons athletes and performers can apply long after the spotlight fades.

To extend this mission beyond books, Pat founded **Former Student Athlete**, a platform created to support athletes and performers navigating life after structured competition. Former Student Athlete provides education, community, and real-world resources focused on financial literacy, career transitions, identity, health, and long-term success once the uniform—or costume—comes off. You can explore this work at:

- www.formerstudentathlete.com
- www.financialliteracyfornil.com
- www.financialliteracyforstudentathletes.com

Pat is easy to find through a Google search, on LinkedIn, or on Twitter, where he regularly shares insights on athletes, performers, money, and life after structured training environments. If you would like to connect with Pat specifically about *Dance Money 101,* you can reach him directly at:

info@dancemoney101.com

Pat's work is rooted in a belief shaped by both football and finance: discipline without direction is fragile, and talent without a plan fades quickly. Dancers deserve a financial playbook as intentional and structured as their training—one that supports stability, freedom, and longevity well beyond the final performance.

Part I: Technique and Foundation

A strong foundation supports every movement.

In dance, technique is everything. Balance, posture, timing, and control are built long before choreography gets complicated. You do not start with turns, leaps, or lifts. You start with placement, alignment, and repetition. The dancers who progress the farthest are not always the most naturally gifted. They are the ones who commit to fundamentals every day.

Money works the same way.

Before you worry about investing, growth, or "making money move," you need a solid base. That base is made up of awareness, structure, and habits. Knowing where your money comes from, where it goes, and how it behaves under pressure matters more than chasing flashy financial moves.

This section focuses on the financial equivalent of technique class. Budgeting, banking, credit, and basic decision-making are not exciting, but they are essential. Poor technique leads to injuries on the floor. Poor financial fundamentals lead to stress, mistakes, and long-term setbacks.

You do not need perfection. You need consistency. Small corrections made early prevent major problems later. Just like in dance, mastery comes from doing the simple things well, over and over again.

Part I is about building control before complexity. When your foundation is solid, everything that follows becomes easier, safer, and more sustainable.

Chapter 1: Why Money Feels Confusing After Dance

Every dancer knows this moment.

You finish class exhausted. Your body hurts, your mind is full, and the correction you keep replaying will not let you rest. You did everything your teacher asked, yet something still feels off. Not bad, just unfinished. Dance trains you to live in that space, always improving, always refining, always chasing cleaner lines and better control.

Money enters your life very differently.

There is no warm-up. No syllabus. No consistent coach. One day you are focused on auditions, rehearsals, and contracts. The next, you are expected to understand rent, taxes, insurance, savings, and long-term planning. No one gathers the company together and says, "Here's how money actually works."

So confusion sets in.

Not because dancers are incapable. But because the system assumes you will figure it out on your own, the same way you learned to survive early mornings, long rehearsals, and late nights. The problem is that money does not reward effort the way dance does. It rewards structure, patience, and consistency.

Why Financial Literacy Is Rarely Taught to Performers

Dance education focuses on mastery of the body and the craft. Time, energy, and identity are poured into technique, performance, and discipline. Financial education rarely fits into that world.

Studios and programs assume money is a separate issue. Companies assume dancers will manage it themselves. Schools focus on training, not life logistics. As a result, many dancers graduate knowing how to execute complex choreography but feeling completely unprepared to manage income that may be inconsistent, seasonal, or unpredictable.

Financial literacy is not ignored because it is unimportant. It is ignored because it feels secondary to survival in the field. Unfortunately, ignoring it early makes everything harder later.

Money Myths Passed Through Studios and Companies

In every dance environment, money myths circulate quietly. They are rarely stated outright, but they shape behavior.

One common myth is that financial stability comes later. That once you "make it," money will sort itself out. In reality, dancers who wait for stability often miss years of opportunity to build a base.

Another myth is that budgeting limits creativity or freedom. Many dancers fear structure because they associate it with restriction. In truth, structure creates freedom. Knowing what you can afford removes constant mental stress.

There is also the belief that struggling financially is part of being a real artist. That instability proves dedication. While sacrifice is real in dance, unnecessary financial chaos does not make you more committed. It only makes life harder.

These myths persist because they are normalized. When everyone around you is stressed about money, it feels inevitable. It is not.

Saving vs Investing vs Gambling

One reason money feels confusing is that different behaviors are often lumped together.

Saving is protection. It is money set aside for stability, emergencies, and short-term needs. It does not aim to grow fast. It aims to be there when needed.

Investing is long-term growth. It involves risk, patience, and time. Investing works when money is allowed to stay untouched and compound.

Gambling is chasing outcomes without a plan. It looks like investing, but it lacks structure, discipline, and risk awareness.

Dancers often confuse investing with gambling because both involve uncertainty. The difference is preparation. Investing is like training for a role over months or years. Gambling is like throwing yourself into choreography you have never rehearsed and hoping it works on stage.

Understanding this difference is foundational. Confusing them leads to frustration, losses, and distrust of the entire financial system.

Why Consistency Beats Chasing Perfection

Dance rewards perfectionism. Clean lines, precise timing, exact placement. That mindset helps you progress technically, but it can sabotage financial decision-making.

Money does not require perfect timing or flawless decisions. It rewards consistent habits. Regular saving, steady contributions, and disciplined behavior over time matter more than one perfect move.

Many dancers delay action because they want the perfect plan. The perfect budget. The perfect moment to start investing. That moment rarely arrives.

Financial progress looks more like daily barre than a flawless performance. Repetition, not intensity, builds strength. Small, imperfect steps taken consistently outperform occasional bursts of effort followed by long gaps.

The Investing Concept Explained Through Dance

In dance, progress comes from fundamentals repeated over time. You do not improve by attempting your hardest choreography every day. You improve by refining basics and stacking progress.

Financially, this works the same way.

Saving is your balance. Investing is your long-term choreography. Risk management is injury prevention. Consistency is rehearsal. When dancers try to skip steps financially, they experience the same problems they would skipping technique class. Injury, burnout, and setbacks.

Money confusion often comes from trying to perform before mastering fundamentals.

Coach's Perspective

What would your dance teacher say if money were part of class?

"Stop rushing."

"Clean it up before adding difficulty."

"Control what you can control."

"Do the basics every day."

"You don't get credit for effort if the execution is sloppy."

A coach would not ask for perfection. They would demand consistency. Show up. Do the work. Build habits you can repeat under pressure.

That same advice applies here.

Game Situations and Decision Points

You get paid from a short contract. Do you spend it all because it feels temporary, or do you save a portion because you know the season ends?

You hear about someone making fast money through a risky opportunity. Do you chase it, or do you ask if it fits your long-term goals?

You feel behind financially and want a quick fix. Do you force a move, or commit to steady improvement?

These decisions mirror rehearsal choices. Shortcutting fundamentals rarely ends well.

Common Dancer Mistakes and Financial Parallels

Dancers often overtrain without rest. Financially, this shows up as overspending without recovery time.

Dancers chase perfection. Financially, this leads to paralysis and inaction.

Dancers compare themselves constantly. Financially, this leads to decisions based on others instead of personal needs.

Recognizing these patterns is the first step toward changing them.

Winning the Long Game

Dance careers are unpredictable. Money should not add unnecessary stress. The dancers who thrive long-term are not the ones who make perfect decisions early. They are the ones who build systems they can maintain.

Financial confidence grows the same way technical confidence does. Through repetition, discipline, and patience.

This chapter is not about doing everything right. It is about understanding why confusion exists and why it is not a personal failure. With the right foundation, clarity replaces anxiety.

Athlete Takeaways

- Clean technique beats flashy choreography every time.
- Consistency builds financial strength faster than perfection.
- Saving protects you. Investing grows you. Gambling exposes you.
- Do not rush difficulty before mastering fundamentals.
- Stack good financial days the same way you stack good rehearsals.

Chapter 2: Know Your Starting Position: Your Financial Snapshot

Every dancer starts rehearsal the same way.

You walk into the studio, find your place, and settle into neutral. Before movement begins, you orient yourself. Where are you in the room? Where is the mirror? Who is around you? What space do you have to work with today?

No choreographer starts teaching phrases without first establishing position.

Money works the same way.

Before you worry about saving more, investing better, or "fixing" anything, you have to know exactly where you are starting from. Most dancers skip this step because it feels uncomfortable, boring, or intimidating. But avoiding your financial starting position does not protect you. It leaves you guessing.

A financial snapshot is not a judgment. It is a reference point. Just like technique class, it tells you what needs work and what is already strong.

Why Avoiding the Snapshot Creates Anxiety

Many dancers feel stressed about money without ever actually looking at the numbers. That stress usually comes from uncertainty, not reality. When you do not know what is coming in, what is going out, or where it is going, your brain fills in the gaps with worst-case scenarios.

Avoidance feels safer in the short term, but it increases long-term pressure.

Looking at your financial snapshot does not make problems worse. It gives them shape. Once something has shape, it can be managed.

Income, Expenses, and Cash Flow

Income is what comes in. Expenses are what go out. Cash flow is the relationship between the two.

For dancers, income is rarely simple. It might include:

- Contracts
- Teaching
- Choreography
- Side jobs
- Stipends
- Seasonal or inconsistent pay

This variability makes cash flow harder to manage, but not impossible.

Positive cash flow means you bring in more than you spend over time. Negative cash flow means you spend more than you earn. Many dancers operate with negative cash flow without realizing it because income arrives in chunks while expenses happen constantly.

Understanding cash flow is like understanding stamina. You may feel fine early in rehearsal, but if you expend energy faster than you recover it, fatigue will catch you later. Money behaves the same way.

Assets, Liabilities, and Net Worth

Assets are things you own that have value. This includes:

- Cash
- Savings
- Investments
- Retirement accounts

- Property

Liabilities are what you owe. This includes:

- Credit cards
- Student loans
- Personal loans
- Other debts

Net worth is simply assets minus liabilities.

Many dancers avoid net worth because they assume it will be negative or disappointing. That assumption misses the point. Net worth is not a score of your worth as a person or artist. It is a measurement tool.

In dance, you use mirrors not to criticize yourself, but to see alignment. Net worth works the same way. It shows balance or imbalance so you can adjust.

Early in a career, net worth is often low or negative. That is normal. What matters is direction, not the number.

Fixed vs Variable Expenses

Expenses fall into two main categories.

Fixed expenses are consistent and predictable. Rent, basic utilities, insurance premiums, minimum debt payments. These are the non-negotiables.

Variable expenses change month to month. Food, transportation, clothing, entertainment, travel, classes, workshops.

Many dancers believe their finances are uncontrollable because income fluctuates. In reality, expenses often fluctuate even more. Variable expenses are where most financial leaks occur.

In dance terms, fixed expenses are your basic technique requirements. Variable expenses are stylistic choices. You cannot eliminate technique, but you can refine how much energy you spend elsewhere.

Understanding which expenses are fixed and which are flexible gives you control without sacrificing quality of life.

Reviewing Where Your Money Actually Goes

This is the most revealing part of the snapshot.

Most people believe they know where their money goes. Very few are accurate without reviewing statements. Small, frequent expenses hide easily. They do not feel significant individually, but collectively they matter.

Reviewing spending is not about shame. It is about awareness.

In rehearsal, watching video can feel uncomfortable, but it is often the fastest path to improvement. Reviewing your spending works the same way. Patterns become obvious. Habits reveal themselves. Adjustments become clear.

You may discover:

- Subscriptions you forgot about
- Spending driven by stress or fatigue
- Costs that no longer align with your priorities

None of this makes you bad with money. It makes you human.

The Investing Concept Explained Through Dance

In dance, you do not build a routine without knowing your current level of strength, flexibility, and control. You assess before you progress.

Financially, your snapshot is that assessment.

Income is your capacity. Expenses are your output. Assets are your stored strength. Liabilities are resistance. Net worth is your overall balance.

Skipping this step is like performing without warming up or knowing the choreography. You might survive, but you will not improve efficiently.

Coach's Perspective

What would a coach say?

"Be honest with yourself."

"The mirror doesn't lie."

"You can't fix what you won't acknowledge."

"Clean up the basics first."

"Know your body before you push it."

A coach would not judge your starting position. They would expect you to own it.

Game Situations and Decision Points

You are offered a short-term contract. Do you review how it fits into your cash flow, or just hope it works out?

You feel behind financially. Do you avoid the numbers, or do you get clear so you can plan?

You want to invest but are unsure if you can afford it. Do you guess, or do you check your snapshot?

Every strong financial decision starts with clarity.

Common Dancer Mistakes and Financial Parallels

Dancers ignore mirrors when frustrated. Financially, this shows up as avoiding bank statements.

Dancers push through fatigue. Financially, this looks like overspending without recovery.

Dancers rely on feeling instead of measurement. Financially, this leads to surprises and stress.

Awareness corrects all of these.

Winning the Long Game

A financial snapshot is not something you do once and forget. It is something you revisit periodically, especially when income, roles, or seasons change.

Just like technique evolves, finances evolve. The dancers who feel most confident with money are not the ones with perfect numbers. They are the ones who know their numbers.

Clarity builds confidence. Confidence creates better decisions. Better decisions compound over time.

Athlete Takeaways

- Know your starting position before adding difficulty.
- Cash flow matters more than income alone.
- Net worth is alignment, not judgment.
- Fixed expenses set the base. Variable expenses shape control.
- Awareness is the first step toward financial strength.

Chapter 3: Finding Balance: Budgeting and Saving

Every dancer understands balance.

Not the kind that looks impressive for a moment, but the kind that holds under pressure. A clean balance is not stiff. It is controlled, responsive, and repeatable. You can get into it consistently, hold it without panic, and exit without falling apart.

That balance does not come from one perfect rehearsal. It comes from repetition, alignment, and trust in fundamentals.

Budgeting and saving work the same way.

Most dancers struggle with money not because they are irresponsible, but because they are trained to tolerate instability. Long hours, inconsistent income, physical exhaustion, and emotional pressure become normal. That environment makes it easy to treat money reactively instead of intentionally.

Financial balance is not about restriction. It is about control.

Why Traditional Budgets Fail Dancers

Many budgeting systems fail dancers because they assume predictable income and routine schedules. Dancers rarely have either.

A rigid, line-by-line budget that expects the same paycheck every two weeks often breaks down immediately. When it fails, dancers blame themselves instead of the system.

A good budget for a dancer must be:

- Flexible
- Simple
- Adaptable to changing income
- Focused on awareness, not perfection

Budgeting is not about forcing your life into a spreadsheet. It is about creating a system that supports how you actually live.

Budgeting Systems That Actually Work

The best budgeting systems for dancers prioritize flow over precision.

One effective approach is category-based budgeting. Instead of tracking every dollar obsessively, you assign broad categories that reflect priorities. Housing, food, transportation, savings, training, discretionary spending.

This allows you to make adjustments without starting over every month.

Another approach is the "pay yourself first" method. Savings comes out automatically, and you live on what remains. This works especially well when income fluctuates, because it turns saving into a habit instead of a decision.

Some dancers prefer percentage-based budgeting. A set percentage goes to essentials, another to savings, and another to flexible spending. When income rises or falls, the proportions stay consistent.

The common thread across all effective systems is this: the system must be sustainable. A budget you abandon is worse than a simple one you follow.

Automating Savings Like Daily Practice

No dancer relies on motivation alone to stay in shape. You build routines. You schedule class. You show up whether you feel inspired or not.

Saving works best the same way.

Automation removes emotion from the process. When savings happen automatically, you are no longer deciding each month whether to save. The decision was already made.

Even small automated savings matter. Just as daily technique class builds over time, small, consistent savings compound into meaningful security.

Automation is not about saving large amounts immediately. It is about creating rhythm. Once rhythm is established, amounts can be adjusted.

Consistency beats intensity.

Emergency Funds as Injury Protection

Every dancer understands injury risk. You warm up, cross-train, and listen to your body not because injury is guaranteed, but because it is possible.

An emergency fund is financial injury protection.

Unexpected expenses will happen. Medical costs, travel issues, broken equipment, sudden income gaps. Without savings, these moments force you into debt or desperation.

An emergency fund creates space. Space to breathe. Space to decide. Space to recover.

It does not need to be perfect. Even a small emergency fund reduces stress dramatically. The goal is not to eliminate risk, but to reduce the damage when something goes wrong.

Just like physical conditioning does not prevent all injuries, savings do not prevent all problems. They shorten recovery time.

Balancing Lifestyle With Long-Term Goals

Dancers are often told to sacrifice now and figure it out later. That mindset can quietly damage financial health.

Balance does not mean eliminating enjoyment. It means aligning spending with values.

If training, wellness, and creative growth matter to you, your money should reflect that. If travel, flexibility, or community matter, they should appear in your budget intentionally, not accidentally.

Problems arise when spending drifts away from priorities. Money leaks into habits that provide short-term relief but long-term regret.

Balancing lifestyle and long-term goals requires honesty. You cannot fund everything fully at the same time. Trade-offs are inevitable. Making them consciously is empowering. Making them accidentally is exhausting.

The Investing Concept Explained Through Dance

In dance, balance comes from alignment, not force.

Financially, budgeting is alignment. Saving is stability. Automation is repetition. Emergency funds are protection.

Trying to "save when you can" is like practicing only when convenient. It leads to inconsistency. Building systems is how professionals operate, both on and off the floor.

Coach's Perspective

What would a coach say?

"Reps matter."

"Do the basics every day."

"Don't rely on adrenaline."

"Control what you can control."

"Consistency wins."

A coach would not expect perfection. They would expect commitment to the process.

Game Situations and Decision Points

You receive a larger-than-usual paycheck. Do you spend it freely or reinforce savings?

Your income drops unexpectedly. Do you panic or lean on your systems?

You feel guilty about saving instead of spending. Do you remember why you started?

These moments reveal whether you have balance or are still reacting.

Common Dancer Mistakes and Financial Parallels

Dancers chase perfection. Financially, this looks like abandoning budgets that are not flawless.

Dancers push through pain. Financially, this shows up as ignoring warning signs.

Dancers rely on bursts of effort. Financially, this leads to inconsistency.

Systems replace stress with structure.

Winning the Long Game

Financial balance is not achieved once. It is practiced continuously.

The dancers who feel most secure financially are not the ones who make the most money. They are the ones who built habits early, adjusted when needed, and stayed consistent even when circumstances changed.

Budgeting and saving are not restrictions. They are tools that allow you to keep dancing longer, with more freedom and less fear.

Athlete Takeaways

- Balance comes from alignment, not force.
- Build a budgeting system you can actually maintain.
- Automate savings to remove emotion.
- Emergency funds reduce recovery time after setbacks.
- Consistency over time creates financial control.

Chapter 4: Credit, Debt, and Financial Missteps

Every dancer knows the moment something goes wrong mid-combination.

You might be moving well. You feel confident. Your body is warm. Then a small mistake happens. A foot slips. A turn travels. Balance wobbles for half a second. Suddenly, everything after that feels rushed. You compensate. You hesitate. What started as a small misstep begins to affect the entire phrase.

Credit and debt work the same way.

When used with awareness and control, they support momentum. When misunderstood or ignored, they quietly interfere with timing, confidence, and long-term progress. Most financial damage does not come from one dramatic mistake. It comes from a series of small decisions made without understanding how credit actually works.

This chapter is about learning how to move through credit and debt without losing control of the choreography.

How Credit Scores and Reports Actually Work

A credit score is not a measure of intelligence or worth. It is a numerical summary of behavior.

It reflects patterns over time, not single moments. Much like a dancer's reputation, it is built quietly through consistency.

Credit scores generally evaluate a few core factors:

- Whether you pay bills on time
- How much of your available credit you use
- How long you have been using credit
- How often you apply for new credit
- The mix of credit types you use

In dance terms, your credit report is the rehearsal footage. Your score is the casting decision based on that footage. You cannot argue with it emotionally. You improve it by adjusting behavior.

Late payments matter more than most people realize. Even one missed payment can disrupt momentum for years. On-time payment is the most powerful movement in the entire sequence.

Credit Cards, Loans, and Interest

Credit cards and loans are tools, not traps by default.

Used well, they create flexibility. Used poorly, they create drag.

Interest is the cost of borrowing time. When you carry a balance, interest compounds quietly, just like fatigue builds when you ignore rest. You may not notice the impact immediately, but over time it affects everything.

Credit cards are best treated like mirrors, not extensions of income. If you cannot pay the balance off consistently, the tool is working against you.

Loans operate similarly, but with longer commitments. Student loans, car loans, and personal loans all trade future income for present access. That trade is not inherently wrong, but it must be intentional.

The danger comes from treating borrowed money as earned money.

Good Debt vs Bad Debt

Not all debt is equal.

Good debt supports long-term growth. It typically:

- Improves earning potential
- Builds durable assets
- Has a clear plan for repayment

Examples include education that increases income or reasonably priced housing that fits your financial reality.

Bad debt primarily funds consumption. It often:

- Covers lifestyle gaps
- Has high interest rates
- Lacks a clear exit plan

In dance terms, good debt is investing in technique, conditioning, or training that expands your career. Bad debt is chasing costumes, trends, or appearances that do not improve performance but leave lasting strain.

The difference is not just interest rate. It is intention and outcome.

Credit Mistakes That Disrupt Momentum

Most financial missteps dancers make with credit come from habits learned under pressure.

Common mistakes include:

- Carrying balances because minimum payments feel manageable
- Opening store cards or promotional financing without understanding terms
- Co-signing for others out of loyalty or pressure
- Ignoring statements because they create anxiety

- Assuming future income will solve current decisions

Dancers are conditioned to push through discomfort. Financially, that instinct can backfire. Avoidance does not stop damage. It delays awareness.

Momentum is not lost in one moment. It is lost through repeated compromises.

The Investing Concept Explained Through Dance

In dance, momentum is built through control, not force.

Financially, credit amplifies whatever habits already exist. Discipline makes credit helpful. Carelessness makes it dangerous.

Debt is not evil. It is weight. Weight can strengthen or strain depending on how it is managed.

The goal is not to avoid credit entirely. The goal is to move through it intentionally without losing balance.

Coach's Perspective

What would a coach say?

"Control your center."

"Don't rush the transition."

"Finish the movement clean."

"Don't add difficulty you can't support."

"Details matter."

A coach would not ban risk. They would demand awareness.

Game Situations and Decision Points

You are offered a credit increase. Do you accept automatically or evaluate your habits first?

You want something now. Do you ask whether it fits your long-term movement or just today's emotion?

Someone asks you to co-sign. Do you understand the full choreography, or just the relationship?

These moments are not dramatic, but they define control.

Common Dancer Mistakes and Financial Parallels

Dancers push through fatigue. Financially, that looks like carrying debt too long.

Dancers ignore small alignment issues. Financially, that becomes ignored balances.

Dancers chase performance moments. Financially, that shows up as spending without structure.

Sustainable careers rely on fundamentals, not adrenaline.

Winning the Long Game

Credit does not determine your future. Habits do.

Dancers who succeed financially treat credit like choreography. They learn it. They respect it. They rehearse discipline until it becomes automatic.

Handled well, credit creates options. Handled poorly, it restricts movement.

The goal is not perfection. It is control, awareness, and the ability to recover quickly from mistakes without losing confidence or direction.

Athlete Takeaways

- Credit reflects patterns, not personality.
- Interest is fatigue you feel later, not now.
- Borrow to support growth, not appearances.
- Small missteps compound if ignored.
- Control the transition to keep momentum.

Chapter 5: The Studio of Money: Banking Basics

Every dancer knows the studio matters.

It is not the most glamorous part of the craft, but it is where everything begins. If the floor is warped, you feel it in your ankles. If the mirrors are cracked, your alignment suffers. If the sound system cuts out, timing falls apart. You cannot perform at a high level if the space where you train is disorganized or unreliable.

Your banking system plays the same role in your financial life.

Most people rush past banking because it feels basic. They want to talk about investing, side income, or big goals. But when your banking setup is sloppy, everything downstream becomes harder. Fees show up unexpectedly. Payments miss. Stress increases. Momentum gets disrupted. Before you can build wealth or plan long term, the studio has to be functional.

Checking vs Savings Accounts

At the most basic level, banking has two core tools: checking accounts and savings accounts. They serve different purposes, and confusing them creates bad habits.

A checking account is for movement. This is where money flows in and out. Paychecks, freelance income, direct deposits, bills, rent, groceries, and everyday spending all run through checking. It is active, high-traffic, and constantly changing.

A savings account is for storage. This is where money sits with intention. Emergency funds, short-term goals, and money you do not want to accidentally spend belong here. Savings should move less often and with purpose.

In dance terms, checking is the studio floor. Savings is the wings. You need both. If everything is on the floor all the time, you crowd the space and increase mistakes. If everything stays in the wings, nothing happens. Separation creates clarity.

Many dancers keep everything in one account and rely on memory to decide what can be spent. That is like rehearsing without marks on the floor. It works until pressure hits. Separate accounts create structure without requiring constant self-control.

Online Banks vs Traditional Banks

Choosing a bank is not about what is best in theory. It is about what works in practice for your life.

Traditional banks offer physical branches, tellers, and face-to-face service. Some dancers value being able to walk in and talk to a person, especially when handling large transactions or resolving issues. There can be comfort in familiarity.

Online banks often offer lower fees, better interest rates on savings, and easy automation. They are built for efficiency. Transfers, alerts, and account management tend to be faster and cleaner.

There is no universally correct choice. The right bank is the one that fits your system and supports your habits.

In dance terms, this is style compatibility. Some dancers thrive in highly structured classical environments. Others do better in flexible, modern settings. Neither is better. Fit matters more than reputation.

What does matter is understanding how your bank works. Know the fee structure. Know transfer timelines. Know how quickly you can access your money in an emergency. Ignorance, not the bank itself, causes most problems.

How Money Moves Electronically

Money does not move magically. It moves through systems with rules, delays, and cutoffs.

Direct deposit sends income straight into your account, often on a set schedule. Electronic transfers move money between accounts, sometimes instantly and sometimes with a delay. Debit cards pull money immediately. Automatic payments run whether you are paying attention or not.

Understanding timing is critical. If rent drafts on the first but income arrives on the second, you can overdraft even if you technically have enough money. If transfers take two days, moving money last minute can cause problems.

In dance terms, this is timing and musicality. The movement itself may be correct, but if you hit it late, the result is still off. Financial mistakes often come from timing, not intent.

Know when money leaves. Know when it arrives. Build buffers so one small delay does not cascade into fees and stress.

Protecting Yourself From Fraud and Overdrafts

Fraud and overdrafts rarely come from dramatic events. They come from inattention.

Protecting yourself starts with awareness. Regularly review your accounts. Not obsessively, but consistently. Know what normal looks like so abnormal stands out quickly.

Set alerts for large transactions, low balances, and unusual activity. These are not annoyances. They are early warning systems.

Keep a buffer in your checking account. Zeroing out your account every month leaves no margin for error. Even a small cushion can prevent fees and panic.

Separate savings from spending. The harder it is to accidentally spend protected money, the safer you are.

In dance terms, this is injury prevention. You warm up not because you expect to get hurt, but because you respect the risk. Clean systems reduce exposure.

Coach's Perspective

If a coach were talking about your banking setup, the message would be blunt.

Handle your basics.

Protect the space.

Details matter.

Do not create your own problems.

No coach cares how beautiful your performance is if you are constantly injured or missing rehearsal. Banking is not exciting, but it is foundational.

Game Situations and Decision Points

You have one account for everything. Do you keep guessing, or do you separate systems and reduce mistakes?

You notice a recurring fee. Do you ignore it because it feels small, or fix the setup and stop the leak?

You see a charge you do not recognize. Do you wait and hope it disappears, or act immediately and protect yourself?

These are small moments, but they compound.

Common Performer Mistakes and Financial Parallels

Dancers ignore boring fundamentals. Financially, that shows up as poor banking habits.

Dancers trust muscle memory without checking alignment. Financially, that shows up as not reviewing statements.

Dancers push through discomfort instead of adjusting technique. Financially, that shows up as living with fees and stress instead of fixing systems.

Winning the Long Game

A clean studio supports growth. You do not think about the floor during a great performance because it is doing its job. Good banking works the same way. When it is set up correctly, it fades into the background and lets you focus on what matters.

Banking will not make you wealthy by itself, but bad banking can keep you stuck.

Athlete Takeaways

- Checking is for movement. Savings is for protection. Keep them separate.
- Choose banks that fit your habits, not someone else's preferences.
- Timing matters. Know when money leaves and arrives.
- Clean systems prevent mistakes before they happen.

- Protect the studio so your financial performance can improve.

Part II: Protection, Longevity, and Career Care

In dance, careers are not built on one great show. They are built on staying healthy, prepared, and available over time. The dancers who last understand recovery, protection, and pacing. They think beyond tonight's performance and make decisions that support tomorrow.

Money works the same way.

Part II is about staying in the game financially. It is not about chasing growth or big wins. It is about protecting what you have already built so one setback does not end the run early. Injury, illness, canceled contracts, slow seasons, or unexpected life changes are part of reality for performers. Financial protection turns those moments from crises into manageable disruptions.

Risk awareness means understanding your limits. It is knowing when to push and when to stay clean. Confidence alone does not equal capacity. Smart dancers and smart money managers respect what can go wrong and plan for it.

Insurance is financial career care. Health insurance protects against medical setbacks. Auto and renters insurance protect day-to-day stability. Homeowners insurance, when relevant, protects years of work. These are not extras. They are foundations.

Life, disability, and liability coverage address bigger risks. For performers, disability insurance is especially important. If your body is your livelihood, protecting income is a professional decision, not a fearful one.

This section is intentionally conservative because longevity requires discipline. Just as you do not dance full out every day, you do not expose your finances to unnecessary risk. You warm up. You recover. You protect yourself so you can keep showing up.

Part II is about staying available for opportunity, adapting when circumstances change, and building a financial life that supports a long, sustainable career, not just one moment in the spotlight.

Chapter 6: Risk Awareness and Career Decisions

In dance, risk is everywhere.

You take risks every time you audition, switch companies, freelance, tour, relocate, or say yes to a contract without knowing what comes next. Some risks move your career forward. Others quietly limit your options later. The difference is not bravery. It is awareness.

Money decisions work the same way.

Most dancers do not fail financially because they are reckless. They struggle because they confuse emotional confidence with financial capacity. You are trained to perform under pressure, to trust yourself, and to take chances. Those traits win roles and open doors. When applied to money without context, they can create exposure you do not see until it matters.

Risk awareness is not about playing small. It is about choosing when risk makes sense and when it does not.

Emotional Risk vs Financial Risk

Emotional risk is how uncertainty feels.

Financial risk is what happens if things go wrong.

Dancers are often comfortable with emotional risk. You are used to rejection, feedback, and competition. Auditions are high-pressure environments with no guarantees. That experience builds confidence and resilience.

Financial risk is different.

If one bad outcome forces you into debt, drains your savings, or limits your ability to say no to the next opportunity, the risk is high, even if you feel confident going in.

In dance terms, this is the difference between attempting a challenging sequence when you have full control versus forcing it when you are fatigued or injured. The move itself might be the same. The context is not.

Confidence does not equal margin.

Time Horizon and Flexibility

Time horizon answers one simple question:

When will you need this money?

Money you need soon must be protected.

Money you do not need for years can tolerate more movement.

Flexibility is the hidden factor.

Do you have savings?

Do you have stable income?

Can you adjust if a contract ends or work slows?

A dancer with multiple income streams and a cash buffer can take more risk than someone living contract to contract with no savings. That is not judgment. That is reality.

Financial decisions should always be filtered through time and flexibility. Ignoring either is how dancers end up locked into situations they cannot exit without damage

How Risk Affects Every Money Decision

Risk is not just about investing.

It shows up in:

- How much cash you keep available
- How much debt you take on

- Whether you commit to long-term leases
- How aggressively you spend during good seasons
- What insurance coverage you carry

Every decision either increases or decreases your ability to adapt.

High-risk choices are not bad by default. They become dangerous when stacked together. Multiple risky decisions at the same time reduce recovery options.

In dance, you would not increase training volume, reduce recovery, and perform at maximum intensity all at once. Financially, the same rule applies.

Knowing When to Take Opportunities and When to Pass

Opportunities are not all equal.

Some move you forward.

Some distract you.

Some cost more than they give.

Saying yes feels productive. Passing feels uncomfortable. Many dancers say yes because they fear missing out or appearing ungrateful. Financially, that mindset can be expensive.

An opportunity should be evaluated on:

- Income stability
- Time commitment
- Impact on health
- Effect on long-term goals
- What you give up by saying yes

Sometimes the smartest move is passing. Not because the opportunity is bad, but because it does not fit the season you are in.

Discipline is choosing alignment over impulse.

Coach's Perspective

A coach would be direct.

Control what you can control.

Know your limits.

Do not force it.

Protect your body and your future.

Make decisions that let you keep training.

Risk is part of growth. Poor awareness is optional.

Just because you can push does not mean you should. Smart careers are built by dancers who understand pacing, not just ambition.

Game Situations and Decision Points

You are offered a short-term contract with uncertain pay.

Do you accept because it sounds exciting, or evaluate whether you can absorb a slow month afterward?

You have a strong season financially.

Do you upgrade your lifestyle immediately, or increase flexibility for the next transition?

You are considering a big purchase.

Do you assess what happens if work slows, or assume momentum will continue?

These decisions feel small in the moment. Over time, they define stability.

Common Dancer Mistakes and Financial Parallels

Dancers trust confidence over context.

Financially, that leads to overcommitment.

Dancers chase momentum.

Financially, that leads to poor timing.

Dancers ignore recovery.

Financially, that leads to burnout and stress.

The same habits that cause injuries shorten financial careers.

Winning the Long Game

Dance careers are unpredictable. Financial lives last decades.

Risk awareness does not eliminate opportunity. It preserves it. The dancers who last understand when to push and when to stay clean. They respect their limits and build systems that absorb setbacks without ending the run.

This is not fear.

This is professionalism.

You are not avoiding risk. You are choosing the right risk at the right time.

Athlete Takeaways

- Confidence is not the same as capacity
- Time horizon and flexibility determine how much risk you can take
- Every money decision affects your ability to adapt
- Not every opportunity deserves a yes
- Long careers are built on smart pacing, not constant intensity

Chapter 7: Insurance Fundamentals Every Dancer Needs

In dance, your body is your instrument.

Your housing, transportation, and personal stability are part of that instrument too, even if they do not feel artistic. When one piece breaks, everything else is affected. Insurance exists to protect the parts of your life that allow you to keep training, performing, and earning.

Most dancers avoid insurance not because it is unimportant, but because it feels confusing, boring, or disconnected from their craft. In reality, insurance is not about fear. It is about continuity. It is what keeps a single setback from turning into a career-altering event.

Insurance does not make you money.

It keeps money problems from ending your momentum.

Health Insurance Basics

Health insurance is the most critical coverage for dancers.

You rely on your body for income. Injuries, overuse issues, and unexpected medical problems are not rare in dance. They are part of the profession. Health insurance determines whether those issues become manageable disruptions or financial crises.

At a basic level, health insurance helps cover:

- Doctor visits

- Physical therapy
- Imaging and diagnostics
- Surgeries and procedures
- Prescription medications

Without coverage, even routine care becomes expensive. With coverage, costs are shared between you and the insurer.

Key concepts to understand:

- **Premium**: what you pay regularly to keep coverage active
- **Deductible**: what you pay out of pocket before insurance starts contributing
- **Copays and coinsurance**: your share of costs after the deductible
- **Out-of-pocket maximum**: the most you pay in a year before insurance covers the rest

Many dancers choose plans based only on monthly premium. That can be a mistake. A low premium with a very high deductible may cost more overall if you actually need care. A higher premium with better coverage may protect you more effectively if injuries are common.

Health insurance is not about hoping you never use it. It is about knowing what happens when you do.

Auto and Renters Insurance

Auto and renters insurance are often overlooked because they feel ordinary. They are anything but.

Auto insurance protects you financially if you cause or are involved in an accident. It can cover:

- Damage to vehicles
- Medical costs
- Legal liability

Driving without proper coverage exposes you to risks that can follow you for years. One accident without insurance can lead to debt, lawsuits, and damaged credit, all of which reduce your ability to relocate or accept new work.

Renters insurance protects what you own and provides liability coverage inside your living space. It is inexpensive and highly valuable.

Renters insurance can cover:

- Personal belongings after theft or damage
- Temporary housing if your unit becomes unlivable
- Liability if someone is injured in your space

Many dancers assume their landlord's insurance protects them. It does not. That policy covers the building, not your belongings or personal liability.

Renters insurance is one of the highest value protections you can buy for the cost.

Homeowners Insurance

If you own a home, homeowners insurance becomes part of your financial foundation.

Homeowners insurance generally covers:

- The structure of the home
- Personal belongings
- Liability for injuries on the property
- Temporary living expenses after damage

Owning property without insurance is not a risk, it is a gamble. A fire, storm, or major repair without coverage can erase years of savings.

Even dancers who do not see themselves as "settled" sometimes buy property. If you do, insurance must be treated as non-negotiable protection, not an optional add-on.

Deductibles, Premiums, and Coverage Limits

Understanding how these elements work together matters more than memorizing definitions.

- **Premiums** are predictable costs. You budget for them.
- **Deductibles** are exposure. You need cash available to handle them.
- **Coverage limits** define how much protection you actually have.

Choosing insurance is about balancing these three factors based on your real life.

Low premiums with high deductibles shift more risk to you.

Higher premiums with lower deductibles shift more risk to the insurer.

There is no universal right answer. The wrong answer is choosing blindly.

As a dancer, ask:

- Can I comfortably cover the deductible if something happens?
- Would a large out-of-pocket cost force me into debt?
- Does this coverage actually match my lifestyle and risks?

Insurance should reduce stress, not create surprises.

Why Dancers Often Underinsure

Many dancers:

- Rely on short-term thinking
- Assume nothing will happen
- Prioritize flexibility over protection
- Avoid recurring expenses

This makes sense emotionally. Financially, it creates exposure.

Underinsurance is not obvious until something goes wrong. Then it is painfully obvious. Injuries, theft, accidents, and liability claims rarely arrive at convenient times.

Insurance is part of career care. It supports longevity the same way recovery, conditioning, and smart scheduling do.

Coach's Perspective

A coach would not frame insurance as optional.

Protect your body.

Protect your ability to train.

Do not let one setback end the season.

Handle your responsibilities like a professional.

You would never perform without warming up. Insurance is a warm-up for life's unpredictability.

Common Dancer Mistakes and Financial Parallels

Dancers assume they are young and healthy.

Financially, that leads to skipping coverage.

Dancers focus only on monthly cost.

Financially, that leads to surprise expenses.

Dancers avoid paperwork and details.

Financially, that leads to uncovered losses.

Avoiding discomfort today often creates pain later.

Winning the Long Game

Insurance does not make headlines. It does not feel artistic or exciting. It is quiet protection that allows you to keep showing up.

The dancers who last are not just talented. They are prepared. They build systems that absorb shocks without ending the run.

Insurance is one of those systems.

You are not buying fear.

You are buying continuity.

Athlete Takeaways

- Insurance protects your ability to keep dancing
- Health coverage is foundational, not optional
- Renters and auto insurance prevent small events from becoming major setbacks
- Deductibles and coverage limits matter more than price alone
- Longevity is built by protecting the basics

Chapter 8: Life, Disability, and Liability Protection

Dance careers are built on movement, timing, and control. You train to manage risk in your body and in your routines. Financial protection works the same way. Life, disability, and liability insurance exist to protect outcomes you cannot rehearse for, but still have to be ready to handle.

Many performers skip these conversations because they feel premature or uncomfortable. Others assume insurance is only for people with families, mortgages, or long careers already behind them. That assumption is one of the most expensive mistakes performers make.

Protection is not about pessimism.

It is about keeping one unexpected event from ending the run.

Term vs Permanent Life Insurance

Life insurance is often misunderstood, especially among younger performers.

At its core, life insurance answers one question.

If something happens to you, who is financially affected and how are they protected?

There are two broad categories.

Term life insurance provides coverage for a specific period of time. If you pass away during that term, a benefit is paid to your beneficiary. If you outlive the term, coverage ends.

Term insurance is:

- Straightforward
- Cost-effective
- Designed to cover real responsibilities for a defined window

For most performers, term insurance is the right starting point. It is used to protect:

- A partner or spouse
- Children
- Parents who depend on your income
- Shared debts like student loans or housing

Permanent life insurance lasts your entire life and includes additional features such as cash value. It is more complex and more expensive.

Permanent insurance is not automatically bad, but it is often sold before it is needed. For performers early in their careers, complexity usually adds cost without adding clarity.

The right question is not which product sounds better.

The right question is what problem you are actually solving.

If no one depends on your income and no shared obligations exist, life insurance may not be urgent. If others rely on you financially, protection matters regardless of age or career stage.

Disability Insurance and Income Protection

Disability insurance is the most important protection most performers do not have.

Your income comes from your ability to perform. Injury, illness, or chronic conditions can interrupt that ability for months or years. Disability insurance replaces a portion of your income if you cannot work.

This is not about catastrophic injury only. Many disabilities are gradual or unexpected. Overuse injuries, surgeries, or health issues can remove you from work even when recovery is expected.

Disability insurance typically:

- Replaces part of your income
- Kicks in after a waiting period
- Continues for a defined time or until recovery

Key things to understand:

- Short-term disability covers temporary interruptions
- Long-term disability covers extended loss of income
- Policies differ in how they define "disabled"

For performers, definitions matter. A policy that only pays if you cannot work at any job is very different from one that pays if you cannot perform your specific role.

Disability insurance is income protection.

Without income, even good budgeting collapses.

Umbrella Liability Coverage

Liability risk is rarely top of mind for performers, but it exists everywhere.

If you cause an accident, injure someone, or are named in a lawsuit, liability coverage protects your assets and future income. Basic policies like auto or renters insurance have limits. Once those limits are exceeded, you are personally responsible.

Umbrella liability coverage sits on top of other policies and provides additional protection.

It is used when:

- Damages exceed basic coverage

- Legal claims escalate
- Multiple parties are involved

Umbrella coverage is relatively inexpensive compared to the protection it offers. It is especially important if you:

- Drive regularly
- Teach, coach, or choreograph
- Host others in your space
- Accumulate savings or investments

As your net worth grows, so does your exposure. Liability coverage protects progress you worked years to build.

Common Insurance Mistakes Performers Make

Performers tend to repeat the same errors.

They assume youth equals safety.

They underestimate income risk.

They avoid paperwork and details.

They buy coverage without understanding it.

They rely on employer coverage that disappears with a contract change.

These mistakes are rarely obvious at first. They show up later, when recovery options are limited.

Insurance gaps do not announce themselves. They reveal themselves under pressure.

How Protection Fits Into Career Longevity

Dance careers rarely follow straight lines. Contracts end. Income fluctuates. Bodies change. Protection creates stability through those transitions.

Life insurance protects people you care about.

Disability insurance protects your income.

Liability insurance protects what you build.

Together, they form a safety net that allows you to take opportunities without reckless exposure.

Protection does not limit ambition.

It supports it.

Coach's Perspective

A coach would not sugarcoat this.

Protect your ability to work.

Do not let one injury end everything.

Handle your responsibilities like a professional.

Plan for what you cannot control.

You train to avoid injury, but you still prepare for it. Financial protection works the same way.

Game Situations and Decision Points

You sign a new contract. Do you reassess coverage or assume nothing changes?

You take on teaching or choreography work. Do you understand your liability exposure?

You build savings. Do you protect it from legal risk?

Each decision compounds over time.

Common Performer Mistakes and Financial Parallels

Performers chase opportunity without protection.

Financially, that leads to fragile success.

Performers rely on optimism.

Financially, that leads to exposure.

Performers delay uncomfortable decisions.

Financially, that leads to forced choices later.

Winning the Long Game

Longevity is not just physical. It is financial.

The performers who last build systems that absorb shocks without ending the run. They respect risk without fearing it. They prepare quietly and consistently.

Life, disability, and liability protection are not about expecting the worst.

They are about making sure the best work you do is not undone by one event.

Athlete Takeaways

- Protect people who depend on you, not just yourself
- Disability insurance protects income, not just health
- Liability coverage protects progress you already earned
- Complexity is not protection, clarity is
- Longevity is built by planning for what you cannot rehearse

Part III: Building Stability and Growth (Investing Fundamentals)

Careers are built with discipline, not shortcuts.

In dance, progress does not come from forcing difficulty too early. It comes from control, repetition, and trust in fundamentals. The same is true with investing.

Investing is not about chasing the flashiest opportunity or trying to outperform everyone else overnight. It is about building stability first, then allowing growth to compound over time. When performers rush this stage, they often take on risk they do not fully understand and lose momentum when things get uncomfortable.

This section focuses on how investing actually works, stripped of hype and shortcuts. You will learn how markets function, what ownership really means, and why patience matters more than timing. Just like in dance, clean execution beats risky tricks.

Stability creates confidence.

Confidence allows growth.

Growth is sustained through discipline.

The goal here is not perfection. It is consistency. When your investing fundamentals are sound, you can handle volatility without panic and opportunity without overreach. That is how financial progress supports a long, healthy career rather than distracting from it.

Think of this section as learning how to stay centered while the tempo changes. You are not trying to win everything at once. You are building a system that holds up over time.

Chapter 9: How Financial Markets Really Work

Financial markets often feel intimidating to dancers because they seem loud, unpredictable, and full of people speaking a language you were never taught. Headlines flash. Prices move. Opinions change daily. It can feel like chaos compared to the structure of a studio, a rehearsal schedule, or a choreographed performance.

But markets are not chaos. They are systems.

Once you understand what the system is designed to do, the noise becomes easier to ignore. Just like dance, the fundamentals matter far more than the flash.

How Markets Function

At their core, financial markets exist to connect people who need capital with people who have capital.

Companies need money to grow. Governments need money to operate. Investors provide that money in exchange for ownership or repayment with interest. Prices move based on expectations about the future, not just what is happening today.

In dance terms, markets are like an audition ecosystem. Choreographers, companies, and productions are constantly evaluating potential. Dancers invest time, training, and effort with the hope of future opportunity. Some projects grow. Some stall. Some fail. The system keeps moving regardless.

Markets are not designed to be comfortable. They are designed to function.

When you understand this, you stop reacting emotionally to every movement and start thinking structurally.

Stocks, Bonds, and Ownership

Stocks represent ownership.

When you buy a stock, you are not buying a symbol on a screen. You are buying a small piece of a real business. That business produces something, hires people, competes, and adapts over time. When it grows, owners benefit. When it struggles, owners feel it.

In dance terms, owning stock is like being part of a company rather than just guest-performing. Your outcome is tied to long-term performance, not one night on stage.

Bonds are different.

Bonds are loans. You lend money to a government or company and receive interest in return. You are not sharing in growth the same way, but you gain predictability.

In dance terms, bonds are like reliable contract work. Not glamorous, but steady. They help cover expenses and reduce uncertainty while you pursue bigger creative goals elsewhere.

Stocks provide growth potential.

Bonds provide stability.

Both matter. Strong careers and strong portfolios use a mix, not extremes.

Ownership Changes the Mindset

One of the biggest misunderstandings dancers have about investing is treating it like speculation instead of ownership.

Speculation is guessing.

Ownership is participation.

Speculation focuses on short-term price movement. Ownership focuses on long-term value creation.

In dance, this is the difference between chasing trends versus developing your craft. Trends come and go. Technique compounds.

Markets reward ownership the same way dance rewards consistency.

Market Cycles and Volatility

Markets move in cycles.

Growth. Slowdown. Decline. Recovery. Repeat.

Volatility is not a flaw in the system. It is part of the system. Prices move because expectations change. News changes. Emotions change. None of this means the system is broken.

In dance terms, volatility is like performance variance. Some shows feel effortless. Others feel off. The existence of bad days does not mean your training failed. It means you are human.

The mistake many people make is confusing volatility with failure.

A price drop does not mean you were wrong. It means the market is repricing expectations. Selling out of fear during volatility is like abandoning technique mid-performance because you felt off balance for one count.

Stability comes from understanding that movement is normal.

Why Long-Term Strategy Wins

Long-term investing is not about predicting the next move. It is about staying in position long enough for fundamentals to matter.

Businesses grow over years, not days. Economies evolve slowly. Compounding takes time.

In dance, careers are built through seasons, not single performances. You do not judge your future based on one audition or one critique. You stay focused on development.

Chasing fast wins in investing is like chasing applause instead of progress. It feels good briefly, but it rarely leads to sustainable success.

Long-term strategy means:

- Staying invested through ups and downs
- Ignoring short-term noise
- Letting time do the heavy lifting

This approach is not exciting. It is effective.

The Trap of Fast Wins

Fast wins are tempting because they promise shortcuts.

Hot stocks.

Trending assets.

"Can't miss" opportunities.

These stories spread the same way unrealistic success stories spread in dance. You hear about someone who "made it overnight" and assume that path is repeatable.

It usually is not.

Fast wins often come with hidden risk. When things go wrong, losses are amplified because there was no foundation underneath.

In dance, skipping fundamentals eventually shows up as injury or inconsistency. In investing, skipping fundamentals shows up as permanent loss.

Coach's Perspective

If a coach were talking about markets, the message would sound familiar.

Do not chase the crowd.

Trust the fundamentals.

Stay consistent.

Control what you can control.

Do not let emotion break form.

Markets reward discipline the same way dance does. The people who succeed are rarely the loudest. They are the most patient.

Game Situations and Decision Points

You see the market drop sharply.

Do you panic and pull out, or remind yourself why you invested?

You hear about a hot opportunity from friends or social media.

Do you chase it, or ask if it fits your long-term plan?

You feel bored with steady progress.

Do you force risk, or stay centered and consistent?

These decisions mirror rehearsal choices every dancer makes. The right answer depends on awareness, not emotion.

Common Dancer Mistakes and Financial Parallels

Dancers chase perfection.

Financially, that becomes chasing timing.

Dancers compare themselves constantly.

Financially, that becomes reactive investing.

Dancers abandon fundamentals under pressure.

Financially, that becomes emotional decision-making.

The same habits that hurt performance hurt finances.

Winning the Long Game

Financial markets are not enemies. They are tools.

Used correctly, they allow your money to work while you focus on your craft, your health, and your career. Used emotionally, they become distractions.

The dancers who build lasting careers understand pacing. They respect cycles. They stay grounded when conditions change.

That same mindset builds long-term financial stability.

You do not need to be brilliant.

You need to be consistent.

Athlete Takeaways

- Markets are systems, not chaos. Learn the structure.
- Stocks mean ownership. Bonds mean stability. Both matter.
- Volatility is normal movement, not failure.
- Fast wins are tempting, but fundamentals last longer.
- Stay disciplined and let time work in your favor.

Chapter 10: Risk, Return, and the Power of Compounding

Every dancer learns early that nothing meaningful comes from one rehearsal.

Strength does not appear after a single class. Balance does not arrive after one correction. Even confidence is built slowly, through repetition, feedback and time. Progress feels invisible for a long stretch, and then one day the movement settles into your body and everything feels different.

Money works the same way.

Risk, return, and compounding are not abstract financial ideas. They are long-term development concepts, no different from technique, conditioning, or artistic growth. The problem is not that dancers misunderstand these ideas. The problem is that no one connects them to a process you already know.

Risk and Reward Tradeoffs

There is no reward without risk.

In dance, choosing higher difficulty always introduces more risk. A bigger jump, a faster turn, or a more complex sequence can elevate a performance, but it also increases the chance of mistakes. Staying simple reduces risk, but it can limit growth.

Money follows the same rule.

Higher potential returns usually come with more uncertainty. Lower-risk choices tend to be steadier but grow more slowly. The mistake many performers make is believing they must always choose one extreme or the other.

In reality, sustainable progress comes from balance.

You do not perform every routine at maximum difficulty. You layer challenge gradually, based on readiness, recovery, and context. Financial decisions should be made the same way. Risk is not something to avoid or chase. It is something to manage.

Emotional Risk vs Financial Risk

One of the most important distinctions to understand is the difference between emotional risk and financial risk.

Emotional risk is how uncomfortable something feels.

Financial risk is how much damage you can actually absorb if things go wrong.

Dancers are used to emotional risk. Auditions, critiques, and performances train you to push through discomfort. That resilience is a strength, but it can also create blind spots with money.

Just because you feel confident taking a risk does not mean your financial situation can support it.

If one bad outcome would force you into debt, limit your choices, or derail your career plans, then the risk is too high, regardless of how bold it feels.

In dance terms, this is attempting difficult choreography while injured because you believe you can push through it. Confidence does not change consequences.

Volatility vs Permanent Loss

Volatility is movement.

Permanent loss is damage.

Markets go up and down. Prices fluctuate. This movement is normal and expected. Volatility is not failure. It is part of how markets function.

Permanent loss happens when poor decisions lock in damage. Panic selling. Overextending. Taking risks you cannot recover from. These are the financial equivalent of ignoring pain until it becomes an injury.

In dance, soreness is normal. Injury is not.

Learning to tolerate volatility without reacting emotionally is one of the most important skills you can develop. Avoiding volatility entirely often leads people to choices that quietly increase long-term risk.

The Power of Compounding Over Time

Compounding is growth building on growth.

Your money earns returns. Those returns earn additional returns. Over time, this creates momentum that accelerates on its own.

The key ingredient is time.

In dance, this is daily practice. Each class reinforces muscle memory. Each correction stacks on the last. You rarely notice progress week to week, but years of consistent work transform your ability.

Compounding works quietly at first. Early progress feels slow. Many people quit before it becomes noticeable. Those who stay consistent are rewarded disproportionately later.

This is why starting matters more than starting perfectly.

Why Consistency Beats Intensity

Many dancers fall into the trap of believing that intensity matters more than consistency. They push hard for short bursts and then burn out or get injured.

Financially, this shows up as:

- Over-investing without a plan
- Taking big risks instead of steady ones
- Starting and stopping based on emotions

Compounding rewards steady effort, not dramatic moves. Small, regular contributions over long periods outperform large, inconsistent ones.

You do not need to be aggressive. You need to be consistent.

The Real Cost of Waiting

Waiting feels safe. It feels responsible. It feels like avoiding mistakes.

In reality, waiting is a decision with consequences.

Every year you delay is a year compounding cannot work for you. That lost time cannot be recovered. Starting later requires more effort to reach the same outcome.

In dance terms, this is skipping foundational training early and trying to make up for it later. Progress is possible, but the path is harder.

You do not need to have everything figured out. You need to begin.

Managing Risk Across Your Life

Risk is not isolated to investing.

It affects:

- How much savings you keep
- How much debt you take on
- What insurance coverage you carry
- How flexible your lifestyle is

A well-managed financial life spreads risk across systems instead of concentrating it in one place. This creates resilience.

In dance, resilience comes from cross-training, recovery, and listening to your body. Financial resilience comes from preparation, balance, and patience.

Coach's Perspective

If a coach were giving advice about money, the message would be familiar.

Control what you can control.

Do not force difficulty before you are ready.

Trust the process.

Stay consistent.

Do not cheat the work.

Compounding rewards discipline, not shortcuts.

Decision Points That Matter

You experience market volatility.

Do you panic or stay the course?

You feel behind financially.

Do you force risk or recommit to consistency?

You want to wait for the perfect moment.

Do you start anyway?

These moments shape outcomes more than any single investment.

Common Dancer Mistakes and Financial Parallels

Dancers rush progress.

Financially, that leads to over-risking.

Dancers ignore recovery.

Financially, that leads to burnout and stress.

Dancers quit when results are slow.

Financially, that means missing compounding.

The same patience that builds artistry builds wealth.

Winning the Long Game

Careers in dance are unpredictable. Financial lives are long.

You cannot control markets any more than you can control casting decisions. What you can control is preparation, discipline, and consistency.

Compounding is not about brilliance. It is about staying in position long enough for progress to show up.

That is how dancers grow.

That is how money grows.

Athlete Takeaways

- Risk and reward are always linked. Balance matters.
- Volatility is normal. Permanent loss is avoidable.
- Compounding rewards consistency, not intensity.
- Waiting costs more than small mistakes.
- Start where you are and keep showing up.

Chapter 11: Stocks Without the Spotlight

In dance, the performers who last are rarely the ones chasing attention every night. They are the ones who understand technique, respect timing, and stay committed to the work even when no one is clapping. They know that longevity is built in rehearsal rooms, conditioning sessions, and quiet consistency, not just on stage.

Stocks work the same way.

Stocks often get treated like the spotlight of personal finance. Headlines focus on dramatic wins, sudden crashes, and stories of people who "made it big." That noise creates the illusion that stock investing is about excitement, speed, and bold moves. In reality, successful stock investing looks much more like a sustainable dance career than a viral performance.

It is patient.

It is disciplined.

And most of the progress happens without applause.

What Owning Stock Actually Means

When you buy a stock, you are not buying a guess, a prediction, or a trend.

You are buying ownership.

Ownership in a real company that operates in the real world. That company sells products or services, hires employees, pays expenses, competes in its industry, and makes long-term decisions. When the company grows and becomes more valuable, your ownership grows. When it struggles, you share that experience as well.

This is a critical distinction many performers miss.

Stocks are not bets on price movement. They are claims on businesses.

In dance terms, owning stock is like committing to a company or long-term project rather than jumping from audition to audition hoping for a quick break. You are aligning yourself with the long-term health of an organization, not just one performance.

This is why time matters so much with stocks. Businesses do not grow in straight lines. They improve, stumble, adapt, and evolve. Owning stock means accepting that process instead of reacting emotionally to every change.

Stocks reward patience because businesses grow over years, not moments.

Why Stocks Feel Uncomfortable to Dancers

Many dancers are trained to seek control.

You train to control your body. You rehearse to reduce mistakes. You aim for precision and repeatability. Stocks can feel unsettling because they move independently of your effort. You can make smart decisions and still see prices fluctuate.

That discomfort leads many performers to believe stocks are gambling.

They are not.

Gambling is chasing outcomes without structure, analysis, or margin for error. Investing in stocks is owning productive assets and letting time and discipline do the work.

The risk with stocks does not come from ownership itself. It comes from impatience, misunderstanding, and emotional decision-making.

Growth vs Value Investing

Two broad approaches help frame how people invest in stocks: growth and value.

Growth investing focuses on companies expected to grow faster than average. These businesses often reinvest profits to expand, innovate, and capture market share. They tend to receive more attention and can feel exciting.

Value investing focuses on companies that appear undervalued relative to their fundamentals. These businesses may not be glamorous, but they often generate steady profits and operate with discipline.

In dance terms, growth investing is high difficulty. More upside, more exposure, more pressure to execute.

Value investing is strong technique. Clean execution, control, and consistency.

Neither approach is inherently better. Most long-term investors benefit from a mix of both. Just as dancers need both technique and expression, portfolios benefit from balance.

Problems arise when performers chase growth exclusively because it feels exciting, or avoid growth entirely out of fear. Longevity comes from blending styles, not choosing sides.

Dividends and Total Return

Dividends are cash payments some companies make to shareholders. They provide income while you hold the stock, regardless of short-term price movement.

But dividends are only part of the story.

Total return includes both price appreciation and income from dividends. Focusing on one while ignoring the other creates an incomplete picture.

In dance, this is like judging a career only by applause or only by consistency. Neither alone tells the full story. Longevity, income stability, opportunity, and growth all matter.

Some stocks deliver most of their return through price growth. Others through steady income. Many provide a combination. What matters is how the total return aligns with your goals, timeline, and tolerance for fluctuation.

Common Investing Myths Performers Hear

Studios, companies, and social media are full of money talk. Much of it sounds confident. Much of it is wrong.

Here are some of the most common myths dancers hear about stocks.

"Stocks are just gambling."

They are not. Gambling relies on chance. Investing relies on ownership, discipline, and time.

"You have to trade constantly to win."

Frequent trading increases stress, taxes, and mistakes. Most long-term success comes from holding, not hopping.

"If the price drops, you failed."

Short-term drops are normal. Permanent loss usually comes from panic, not patience.

"You need inside information."

Public companies disclose information for everyone. Consistency matters more than secrets.

"If you didn't buy at the bottom, it's too late."

Waiting for perfect timing often means never starting. Progress beats perfection.

These myths thrive because they are emotional and simple. Real investing is neither. It is structured, patient, and often boring.

Boring works.

Why Chasing the Spotlight Causes Financial Injury

Stocks become dangerous when treated like performance opportunities.

This shows up as:

- Buying because something is popular
- Selling because prices dropped suddenly
- Jumping strategies out of boredom
- Treating investing as entertainment

In dance, this is chasing trends instead of building technique. It may look exciting, but it rarely creates a sustainable career.

Markets reward discipline, not drama.

The most successful investors are often invisible. They hold quality assets, stay invested through uncertainty, and resist the urge to react emotionally.

Stocks Are Not Meant to Be Traded Like Rehearsal Corrections

Many people believe success with stocks requires constant adjustment.

That belief comes from noise, not results.

In dance, you do not overhaul technique after every note. You trust the process, refine gradually, and stay consistent. Investing works the same way.

Effective stock investing usually means:

- Buying with intention
- Holding through cycles
- Reviewing periodically, not daily
- Adjusting when fundamentals change, not emotions

Patience is not passive. It is a disciplined strategy.

The Role of Stocks in a Balanced Financial Life

Stocks are powerful, but they are not meant to stand alone.

They work best alongside:

- Cash for stability
- Bonds for balance
- Insurance for protection
- Career income for flexibility

Expecting stocks to solve every financial challenge creates unnecessary pressure. Used correctly, they support long-term growth while other systems provide support.

In dance terms, stocks are not the entire routine. They are one element, executed cleanly within a complete program.

Coach's Perspective

A coach talking about stocks would not hype excitement.

They would reinforce fundamentals.

Stay consistent.

Trust the process.

Do not chase attention.

Control what you can control.

Do not abandon the plan after one bad rehearsal.

Discipline beats drama.

Winning the Long Game

Stocks are not lottery tickets.

They are tools for building ownership in productive businesses over time. When treated with patience and discipline, they quietly compound progress. When treated emotionally, they create stress and mistakes.

You do not need to be brilliant.

You need to stay committed.

That mindset has already served you in dance. It works just as well with money.

Athlete Takeaways

- Owning stock means owning real businesses, not chasing trends
- Growth and value both matter. Balance builds longevity
- Dividends plus price growth equal total return
- Spotlight chasing leads to emotional mistakes
- Discipline and patience create lasting financial careers

Chapter 12: Bonds and Maintaining Stability

In dance, stability is rarely celebrated, but it is always required.

Audiences notice leaps, turns, and dramatic moments. They do not applaud balance checks, core engagement, or clean landings. Yet without those elements, the routine falls apart. The dancer who lasts understands that stability is not the absence of movement. It is the control that allows movement to happen safely and consistently.

Bonds play that role in a financial life.

They are not exciting. They do not generate headlines. They rarely become conversation starters. But they provide structure, predictability, and control when everything else feels unstable. Bonds are not designed to steal the spotlight. They exist to keep the routine from breaking down.

How Bonds Work

At their core, bonds are simple.

A bond is a loan.

When you buy a bond, you are lending money to a government, a municipality, or a company. In exchange, the borrower agrees to pay you interest over a set period of time and return your original money at maturity.

That is it.

There is no ownership like with stocks. You are not participating in upside growth. You are acting as a lender, not a partner.

In dance terms, bonds are the supportive structure beneath the movement. They do not drive expression, but they make expression possible by reducing instability.

Bonds are built around predictability:

- Predictable income through interest payments
- Predictable timelines through maturity dates
- Predictable expectations about return of principal

This predictability is why bonds are often misunderstood. People assume boring equals useless. In reality, boring often equals reliable.

Why Bonds Feel Unnecessary Early On

Many dancers struggle to appreciate bonds because of where they are in their careers.

Early in a dance career, income may be inconsistent. Opportunities may feel fragile. Time horizons feel long. In those moments, growth feels urgent and stability feels secondary.

That mindset is understandable.

But dismissing bonds entirely is like ignoring conditioning because you want to rehearse choreography. It works until fatigue or injury shows up.

Bonds are not about maximizing return. They are about managing risk.

They exist to reduce volatility, create income, and protect the routine when conditions change.

Interest Rate Risk and Credit Risk

Bonds come with risks, just like dance comes with physical strain.

Two risks matter most.

Interest rate risk means bond prices can move when interest rates change. When rates rise, existing bonds with lower interest payments become less attractive, and their prices can fall. When rates fall, existing bonds may increase in value.

Credit risk means the borrower might fail to repay the loan. Governments and large, stable companies tend to have lower credit risk. Smaller or financially weaker borrowers usually offer higher interest to compensate for higher risk.

In dance terms, this is like choosing difficulty and tempo. Higher difficulty increases risk. Slower, cleaner execution reduces it.

Higher bond yields often come with higher credit risk. Lower risk bonds usually offer lower returns.

There is no free stability.

Understanding this tradeoff is more important than memorizing bond mechanics. Bonds are not risk-free. They are risk-managed.

When Bonds Make Sense

Bonds matter most when stability matters.

They often play a larger role when:

- You are closer to needing the money
- You want predictable income
- You need to reduce overall portfolio swings
- You are protecting progress you have already made

This is why bonds become more important over time. Early in a career, growth may matter more. As goals approach, protection matters more.

In dance, this is adjusting choreography to match stamina, injury history, and performance demands. You do not perform the same routine at every stage of your career. You evolve to protect longevity.

Financial routines work the same way.

Bonds allow you to stay invested without feeling forced to react emotionally when markets move. They reduce pressure, not opportunity.

Stability Does Not Mean Standing Still

One of the biggest misunderstandings about bonds is believing they prevent progress.

They do not.

Bonds allow progress to continue without unnecessary stress. They create a counterbalance to the volatility of stocks.

In a diversified portfolio:

- Stocks drive growth
- Bonds provide stability
- Cash provides flexibility

Each element serves a different purpose. Removing bonds entirely is like removing balance work from training. You may feel more powerful at first, but breakdown becomes more likely.

Stability does not slow growth. It protects it.

Bonds in a Diversified Portfolio

Diversification is not about owning more things. It is about owning different types of risk.

Stocks and bonds respond differently to economic conditions. When stocks experience sharp declines, bonds often hold value or decline less. That relationship smooths the overall experience.

This matters more than people realize.

Most investing mistakes happen under emotional pressure. Bonds reduce that pressure by limiting how extreme portfolio swings feel.

In dance terms, bonds are the quiet moments that allow the audience to breathe. Without them, intensity becomes overwhelming and unsustainable.

Diversification is not about maximizing returns in the best year. It is about surviving and progressing through all years.

Why Bonds Are Often Abandoned at the Wrong Time

Many people abandon bonds when markets are strong.

Stocks are rising. Confidence is high. Stability feels unnecessary. That is usually when bonds are most important.

The decision to reduce stability often happens right before volatility increases.

In dance, this is pushing through fatigue because you feel good in rehearsal, only to break down on performance day.

Stability should be built when conditions are calm, not added after stress appears.

Coach's Perspective

A coach would not hype bonds.

They would normalize them.

Stay balanced.

Protect your base.

Do not sacrifice control for flash.

Longevity matters.

Do not let one mistake end the routine.

Bonds are not exciting. They are essential.

Bonds Are Not About Fear

Using bonds does not mean you are scared of growth.

It means you respect risk.

Fear reacts. Discipline plans.

Bonds allow you to stay committed to long-term investing without panic. They reduce the chance that you abandon your plan during difficult moments.

They do not replace stocks. They support them.

Winning the Long Game

Careers end. Bodies change. Opportunities shift.

Financial stability allows you to adapt without desperation.

Bonds are not designed to make you rich quickly. They are designed to keep you stable enough to keep moving forward.

That stability is what allows dancers to transition, evolve, and sustain success beyond one performance.

Quiet strength lasts longer than loud momentum.

Athlete Takeaways

- Bonds are loans, not bets
- Stability protects progress when conditions change
- Interest and credit risk are tradeoffs, not surprises
- Bonds balance growth rather than replace it
- Longevity is built on control, not constant intensity

Chapter 13: Funds, ETFs, and Ensemble Investing

No dancer succeeds alone.

Even soloists rely on choreographers, teachers, musicians, stage crews, and ensemble members to create a complete performance. The audience may focus on one person in the spotlight, but the success of the piece depends on coordination, timing, and trust across the entire group.

Investing works the same way.

While individual stocks can feel like starring roles, most long-term financial success is built through ensemble investing. Mutual funds and ETFs allow you to invest as part of a coordinated group rather than trying to carry the entire performance yourself.

This chapter is about understanding how those ensembles work, how to choose between them, and how to avoid complexity that quietly undermines progress.

What Mutual Funds and ETFs Actually Are

At a basic level, both mutual funds and ETFs are collections of investments bundled together into a single vehicle.

Instead of owning one stock or one bond, you own a slice of many at the same time.

That is the core value.

Mutual funds pool money from many investors and are typically bought or sold once per day at the fund's closing value.

ETFs, or exchange-traded funds, also pool investments but trade throughout the day like stocks.

The mechanics differ, but the purpose is the same: diversification through structure.

In dance terms, these funds are ensembles. They distribute responsibility across many performers instead of relying on a single move to carry the routine.

Why Ensemble Investing Matters

Trying to pick individual winners feels empowering. It feels skill-based. It feels like control.

But over time, concentration increases risk.

If one investment fails, the damage can be severe. Ensemble investing reduces the impact of any single mistake by spreading exposure across many companies, industries, or asset types.

This is not about lowering standards. It is about protecting outcomes.

In dance, an ensemble absorbs mistakes. One dancer slipping does not end the performance. In a solo, it can.

Funds provide that same buffer.

Index Strategies vs Active Strategies

Once you understand funds, the next decision is how they are managed.

Index strategies are designed to track a specific market index. They aim to match performance, not beat it.

Active strategies involve managers trying to outperform the market through selection and timing.

Both approaches exist in dance.

Index investing is like performing a well-established repertory piece. The choreography is known. The structure is proven. Success comes from execution, not reinvention.

Active investing is like creating new choreography. It can be powerful, but it introduces additional risk. Not every experiment succeeds, and mistakes are more costly.

Over long periods, most active strategies struggle to consistently outperform index strategies after costs. That does not mean active investing is wrong. It means it must justify its complexity.

Simplicity often wins because it is easier to sustain.

Fees and Expense Ratios

Fees are the most overlooked threat to long-term success.

They are quiet. They feel small. They rarely trigger emotional reactions. But over time, they compound against you.

Every fund charges an expense ratio, which is the annual cost of managing the fund expressed as a percentage. That cost comes out of returns before you ever see them.

A small difference in fees may not matter in one year. Over decades, it can significantly reduce outcomes.

In dance terms, fees are inefficient transitions. Each one barely registers, but together they drain energy and weaken the final performance.

You do not need the cheapest option available. You do need to understand what you are paying and why.

High fees demand high value. If that value is unclear, the cost is likely unnecessary.

Diversification Without Complexity

Many investors confuse diversification with complication.

They believe owning more funds automatically improves results. In reality, too many overlapping investments often reduce clarity without adding protection.

True diversification means owning assets that behave differently, not owning dozens of versions of the same thing.

You do not need a massive ensemble. You need a balanced one.

In dance, adding dancers does not improve a piece if they all perform the same role. Balance comes from contrast, spacing, and coordination.

The same is true financially.

A small number of well-chosen funds can provide broad diversification across:

- Companies
- Industries
- Geographies
- Asset types

More complexity does not equal more control. It often creates confusion that leads to poor decisions.

Why Funds Reduce Emotional Mistakes

One of the greatest advantages of funds is emotional insulation.

Individual investments invite overreaction. News headlines, short-term performance, and social comparison can trigger unnecessary changes.

Funds smooth those emotional swings.

When one holding struggles, others may perform well. That balance reduces the urge to intervene at the wrong time.

In dance, this is trusting the choreography rather than improvising under pressure. Discipline preserves quality.

Most investing failures are not caused by bad markets. They are caused by abandoning plans during stressful moments.

Funds help you stay in the routine.

When ETFs Offer Additional Flexibility

ETFs offer some features that appeal to certain investors:

- Intraday trading
- Greater tax efficiency in some structures
- Transparency of holdings

These features matter more for experienced investors or specific strategies. For most long-term goals, the difference between mutual funds and ETFs is less important than consistency and cost.

Choosing between them is less about superiority and more about fit.

What matters most is using the structure correctly, not optimizing every detail.

Common Ensemble Investing Mistakes

Many dancers struggle with ensemble investing because it feels less personal.

Common mistakes include:

- Chasing the hottest fund after strong performance
- Overloading on similar funds that overlap heavily
- Ignoring fees because results look good temporarily
- Abandoning diversified strategies during downturns

These mistakes mirror performance habits.

Chasing applause instead of execution. Changing choreography mid-show. Focusing on one review instead of the full season.

Consistency beats improvisation.

Coach's Perspective

A coach would say:

Trust the system.

Know your role.

Do not try to do everything yourself.

Clean execution beats flashy mistakes.

Stay disciplined when momentum shifts.

Funds are systems, not shortcuts.

They reward patience, repetition, and adherence to the plan.

Ensemble Investing and Career Longevity

Dance careers are unpredictable. Income fluctuates. Opportunities change. Transitions happen.

Ensemble investing supports long-term adaptability. It allows growth while managing uncertainty.

You do not need to predict the future. You need a structure that works across many futures.

Funds provide that structure.

They do not guarantee success. They increase the odds that consistency leads to progress.

Winning the Long Game

The strongest financial performances rarely rely on one perfect choice.

They rely on systems that absorb mistakes, adapt to change, and keep moving forward.

Ensemble investing is not about settling for average. It is about creating stability that allows excellence to compound over time.

That is how careers last. That is how financial lives grow.

Athlete Takeaways

- Funds spread responsibility across many investments
- Index strategies emphasize discipline over prediction
- Fees quietly compound against you over time
- Diversification works best when it stays simple
- Strong systems outperform solo efforts over long careers

Chapter 14: Real Estate and Alternative Paths

Not every successful dance career follows the same path.

Some dancers move through traditional companies. Others freelance, tour, teach, choreograph, or build studios of their own. Some stay close to the stage. Others transition behind the scenes. There is no single "right" path, only paths that fit the body, timing, and goals of the dancer.

Money works the same way.

Real estate and alternative investments are often presented as advanced moves or "next-level" strategies. They are not inherently better or worse than traditional investing. They are simply different paths, each with their own demands, risks, and tradeoffs. Understanding when they fit and when they do not is far more important than chasing them because they sound impressive.

This chapter is about clarity, not hype.

Renting vs Owning: Control, Flexibility, and Commitment

The decision to rent or own property is often emotional. Owning is marketed as adulthood, stability, and success. Renting is sometimes framed as temporary or falling behind.

That framing is misleading.

Renting offers flexibility. It allows you to relocate for contracts, tours, residencies, or teaching opportunities without being anchored to a property. For dancers whose income and location can change quickly, flexibility is not a weakness. It is protection.

Owning offers control and long-term stability. You build equity over time, lock in housing costs, and gain a sense of permanence. That can be valuable once income is more predictable and location is settled.

Financially, neither option is automatically better.

Owning comes with hidden costs: maintenance, repairs, taxes, insurance, and time. Renting removes many of those responsibilities but does not build equity.

In dance terms, renting is like freelancing. Owning is like committing to a company contract. Both can work. Both require honesty about readiness and goals.

The mistake is choosing one because it feels expected, not because it fits your current stage.

Real Estate as an Investment, Not a Lifestyle Choice

When real estate becomes an investment rather than a residence, the analysis must change.

An investment property is a business. It has cash flow, expenses, risk, and management demands. It is not passive just because someone else lives there.

Many people underestimate the work involved. Repairs do not respect rehearsal schedules. Tenants do not care about show weeks. Vacancies, legal issues, and unexpected costs can arrive at inconvenient times.

Real estate can be a powerful tool, but it concentrates risk. One property in one location exposes you to local market conditions, tenant behavior, and timing risk.

That concentration can be manageable. It just needs to be acknowledged.

In dance, this is like building a career around one company or one style. It can be rewarding, but it carries dependency risk.

REITs and Indirect Ownership

For those who want exposure to real estate without direct management, Real Estate Investment Trusts, or REITs, offer an alternative.

REITs are companies that own or finance income-producing real estate. When you invest in a REIT, you own a share of a portfolio of properties rather than a single building.

This structure provides diversification, liquidity, and simplicity.

You can buy and sell REITs easily, often within traditional investment accounts. You avoid maintenance, tenant issues, and operational decisions.

The tradeoff is control. You do not choose the properties. You accept market pricing and management decisions.

In dance terms, REITs are like joining a touring ensemble rather than running your own studio. You participate in the outcome without handling the logistics.

For many dancers, REITs provide a cleaner, more flexible way to include real estate exposure without overcommitting resources or time.

Alternative Investments: What They Really Are

The term "alternative investments" covers a wide range of assets outside traditional stocks and bonds.

Common examples include:

- Commodities
- Private equity
- Private real estate funds
- Hedge strategies
- Collectibles

These investments are often marketed as sophisticated or exclusive. In reality, they are tools with specific use cases.

Alternatives can offer diversification because they may behave differently than traditional markets. They can also introduce new risks, including lack of transparency, limited liquidity, higher fees, and complexity.

Many alternatives require long lock-up periods. Once invested, your money may be inaccessible for years.

This matters deeply for dancers, whose income and opportunities can change quickly.

In performance terms, alternatives are high-difficulty choreography. They may add value in the right routine. They can also increase the chance of mistakes if added without sufficient preparation.

Liquidity: The Often-Ignored Constraint

Liquidity refers to how easily you can access your money without penalty or delay.

This is one of the most important considerations for performers.

Emergency expenses, career transitions, injuries, relocations, and unexpected opportunities all require access to cash. Investments that look attractive on paper can become liabilities if they trap money when you need it most.

Real estate and many alternatives are illiquid. Selling takes time. Pricing can be uncertain. Exiting quickly often means accepting losses.

Liquidity is not about fear. It is about adaptability.

In dance, this is having the freedom to step away from a project that is not right, or to accept one that suddenly appears. Financial rigidity limits artistic and career freedom.

Risk Concentration vs Risk Spreading

Traditional portfolios spread risk across many assets. Real estate and alternatives often concentrate risk into fewer positions.

That concentration can amplify both gains and losses.

Owning one property or one private investment means outcomes hinge on fewer variables. When things go well, results can be strong. When things go poorly, recovery is harder.

This is not a reason to avoid these paths. It is a reason to size them appropriately.

In dance, you do not build an entire season around one performance. You pace energy across many shows.

Financial exposure should be paced the same way.

Common Mistakes Performers Make With Alternatives

Several patterns show up repeatedly:

- Investing in real estate too early, before income stabilizes
- Underestimating time and emotional demands
- Locking up money needed for flexibility
- Chasing alternatives because others are doing it
- Ignoring fees and complexity

These mistakes often stem from comparison and impatience.

Alternatives are not upgrades. They are tools. Tools only work when used correctly.

Coach's Perspective

A coach would be direct:

Know what you are signing up for.

Do not sacrifice balance for ego.

Respect the demands of the routine.

Control risk before chasing difficulty.

Stay flexible.

The best dancers choose paths that support longevity, not applause.

Choosing the Right Path for You

Real estate and alternative investments can play a role in a well-structured financial life. They can also create stress if introduced too early or too heavily.

The right question is not "Is this a good investment?"

The right question is "Is this the right investment for me right now?"

Timing matters. Capacity matters. Flexibility matters.

There is no universal sequence. There is only alignment between resources, goals, and reality.

Winning the Long Game

Careers in dance are marathons built from many transitions. Financial decisions should support that reality, not restrict it.

Real estate and alternative paths can add depth and resilience when chosen intentionally. They can also reduce freedom when chosen prematurely.

Success comes from matching strategy to stage, not copying someone else's choreography.

Athlete Takeaways

- Renting and owning serve different career stages
- Real estate concentrates risk and requires commitment
- REITs offer diversified real estate exposure with flexibility
- Alternatives add complexity and reduce liquidity
- The right path supports longevity, not comparison

Part IV: Adjustments, Transitions, and Sustainability

Successful careers adapt without losing form.

No dance career stays static.

Roles change. Bodies change. Companies change. Opportunities appear and disappear. What separates dancers who last from those who burn out is not talent alone. It is the ability to adjust without losing fundamentals.

Money follows the same pattern.

This part of the book focuses on adaptation. Not reaction. Not panic. Thoughtful, intentional adjustments that keep you moving forward even as circumstances shift.

Why Adjustments Matter More Than Big Moves

Early in a career, progress often comes from big changes. New training environments. New teachers. New companies. Over time, success depends less on dramatic shifts and more on small, well-timed adjustments.

Financially, this means:

- Tweaking systems instead of blowing them up
- Making changes based on reality, not emotion
- Updating plans as income, goals, and responsibilities evolve

Overreacting creates instability. Refusing to adjust creates stagnation.

Sustainable careers live in the middle.

Transitions Are Not Failures

Dancers transition constantly. From student to professional. From company to freelance. From performer to teacher, choreographer, director, or something entirely different.

Financial transitions follow the same rhythm.

- Income changes
- Benefits come and go
- Expenses shift
- Priorities evolve

None of this means something went wrong.

Problems arise when financial systems are built for one version of life and never updated. What worked during a full-time contract may not work during freelancing. What worked with roommates may not work when supporting others.

Adapting systems is not quitting. It is professionalism.

Sustainability Is a Financial Skill

Longevity is not just physical. It is financial and mental.

Sustainable money systems:

- Reduce stress during slow periods
- Create flexibility during career pivots
- Support recovery from injuries or burnout
- Allow you to say no when something is not right

Unsustainable systems force dancers into choices they would not otherwise make. Accepting unsafe work. Staying in bad environments. Delaying recovery.

Money should support the career, not control it.

Keeping Form While You Adjust

Adjustments should never abandon fundamentals.

That means:

- Maintaining savings habits
- Avoiding unnecessary debt
- Staying insured and protected
- Reviewing plans regularly

In dance, you do not sacrifice technique to survive a tough season. You return to it.

Financial discipline works the same way.

The Goal of This Section

Part IV is about learning how to move through change without losing balance.

Careers end when dancers stop adapting or adapt recklessly. Financial stability disappears the same way.

Sustainability is not about staying comfortable. It is about staying prepared.

Careers that last are built by dancers who know when to shift weight, when to pause, and when to keep moving forward with control.

Chapter 15: Asset Allocation and Financial Balance

In dance, balance is never static. It is not something you achieve once and hold forever. Balance is constantly adjusted. Weight shifts. Muscles engage and release. Small corrections happen in real time so the movement stays controlled instead of collapsing.

Asset allocation works the same way.

Asset allocation is simply how your money is divided across different types of investments, most commonly stocks, bonds, and cash. It is not about picking the perfect investment. It is about deciding how much risk, stability, and flexibility you are carrying at any given stage of your career and life.

Most financial mistakes are not caused by bad investments. They are caused by poor balance.

Stocks, Bonds, and Cash: The Core Trio

Every portfolio is built on three core elements.

Stocks represent growth. When you own stocks, you own pieces of companies. Over time, stocks have historically provided the highest returns, but they also come with the most volatility. They move. Sometimes dramatically.

In dance terms, stocks are dynamic movement. Jumps, turns, big traveling phrases. They create momentum and progress, but they require strength and control to execute safely.

Bonds represent stability. Bonds are loans you make to governments or companies in exchange for interest. They tend to fluctuate less than stocks and provide steadier returns, though usually lower over long periods.

Bonds are control work. Centering exercises. Grounded movement. They do not draw attention, but they keep the body organized and supported.

Cash represents flexibility. Cash does not grow much, but it is available immediately. It allows you to respond to opportunities, emergencies, and transitions without stress.

Cash is stillness. The pause before movement. The breath that lets you reset without falling out of form.

Balance comes from using all three intentionally. Too much movement without control creates chaos. Too much control without movement limits growth. Too much stillness prevents progress.

Why Balance Matters More Than Performance

Many dancers carry a performance mindset into investing. They want the best return. The fastest growth. The highest number.

That is like judging a career based on one performance instead of longevity.

A portfolio that grows quickly but cannot survive downturns will eventually break. A portfolio that is too conservative may feel safe but quietly fail to keep up with long-term needs.

Asset allocation is about sustainability. It is not designed to win one moment. It is designed to keep you progressing across decades.

Domestic vs International Exposure

Just as dancers train in different styles and traditions, companies operate all over the world.

Domestic investments focus on companies based in your home country. International investments include companies based outside it.

Relying only on domestic exposure is like training in one studio, one style, one choreographer's vocabulary. It can work, but it limits perspective and opportunity.

International exposure adds diversification. Different economies grow at different times. Political systems, consumer behavior, and innovation cycles vary globally. When one region struggles, another may thrive.

You do not need to know which country will outperform next. You only need to avoid putting everything in one place.

Financial balance comes from spreading exposure, not predicting outcomes.

Diversification Is Not About Complexity

Diversification simply means not relying on one thing to carry everything.

In dance, no single muscle group does all the work. In performance, no single dancer carries an entire ensemble. In training, no single exercise builds complete strength.

Financially, diversification means spreading money across:

- Different asset types
- Different industries
- Different regions

This reduces the impact of any one failure.

Diversification does not require dozens of accounts or constant trading. It requires intentional structure.

The goal is not to eliminate risk. The goal is to prevent one mistake or downturn from ending the performance entirely.

Career-Stage Allocation

Your asset allocation should change as your career changes.

Early in a career, time is your biggest advantage. You can recover from market downturns. You have more years for growth to compound. This often allows for a higher emphasis on stocks.

That does not mean reckless risk. It means acknowledging that volatility matters less when you are not relying on the money yet.

Mid-career brings complexity. Income may rise, but responsibilities often increase. Housing decisions, family considerations, and career transitions require more stability and flexibility.

Allocation often shifts here. Still growing, but with more balance and protection.

Later stages emphasize preservation and income. The focus becomes maintaining what you have built and drawing from it thoughtfully. Stability matters more because recovery time is shorter.

None of these stages are rigid. They overlap. Freelancers may cycle through them multiple times. Injuries, career pivots, and new opportunities all affect timing.

The key is awareness.

Common Balance Mistakes Dancers Make

Many dancers make the same financial mistakes they would never tolerate in training.

One is chasing difficulty too early. Investing aggressively without savings, insurance, or stability is like attempting advanced choreography without a warm-up. It may work briefly, but the risk of injury is high.

Another is freezing in fear. Avoiding growth because of volatility is like refusing to leave the barre. Safe, but limiting.

Some dancers never adjust. They set a portfolio once and ignore it as life changes. That is like dancing the same role forever while the choreography evolves around you.

Balance requires engagement.

Coach's Perspective

A coach would not overcomplicate this.

They would say:

- Know your role right now
- Do not force movement that is not ready
- Stay strong in the fundamentals
- Adjust as the routine evolves

Financial balance is not about showing off. It is about staying upright under pressure.

Game Situations and Decision Points

You receive a raise or new contract. Do you adjust your allocation or keep everything the same?

Markets drop sharply. Do you abandon your plan or stay balanced?

Your career shifts from company work to freelance. Does your money reflect that change?

These are not theoretical questions. They are real moments where balance either holds or collapses.

Winning the Long Career

Great dancers do not rely on perfect conditions. They rely on control, awareness, and adaptability.

Asset allocation is the financial expression of those same traits.

When your money is balanced, you make decisions from clarity instead of fear. You can take opportunities without panic. You can handle setbacks without falling apart.

Balance does not eliminate uncertainty. It gives you the strength to move through it.

Athlete Takeaways

- Growth, stability, and flexibility all have a role. Balance them.
- Diversification protects careers the way technique protects bodies.
- Your allocation should evolve as your career evolves.
- Do not chase difficulty before fundamentals are secure.
- Sustainable balance keeps you performing long after the spotlight fades.

Chapter 16: Buying, Holding, and Trusting the Process

In dance, progress is rarely dramatic in the moment. You show up. You repeat combinations. You correct small details that no one in the audience will ever notice. Most days feel ordinary. Improvement happens quietly, over time, because you trusted the process instead of chasing constant validation.

Investing works the same way.

This chapter is not about finding the perfect investment or timing the market perfectly. It is about execution. Opening the right accounts, funding them consistently, choosing simple tools, and then having the discipline to stay the course when emotions try to pull you off balance.

Most long-term financial success is not built on brilliance. It is built on patience.

Opening and Funding Accounts

Before you can invest, you need the right containers.

Accounts are not investments themselves. They are structures that determine how your money is taxed, accessed, and protected. Opening the right accounts is like choosing the right studio, floor, and shoes before rehearsal even begins.

Common investing accounts include:

- Employer retirement plans
- Individual retirement accounts
- Taxable brokerage accounts

Each serves a different purpose. Some are designed for long-term retirement. Some allow flexibility for future goals. Some provide tax advantages if rules are followed.

The biggest mistake dancers make is delaying account setup because it feels intimidating or technical. In reality, opening an account is often easier than registering for a class or audition. The complexity comes later, and even then, it is manageable.

Funding matters more than perfection. A modest account funded consistently will outperform a perfectly designed account that never receives money.

Repetition builds results.

Market Orders vs Limit Orders

When you buy investments, you place orders. The two most common types are market orders and limit orders.

A **market order** buys or sells an investment at the current market price. It prioritizes execution over precision. You get in quickly, accepting whatever the current price is.

A **limit order** sets a specific price you are willing to pay or receive. It prioritizes price control over immediacy. The trade only happens if the market reaches your chosen price.

In dance terms, this is the difference between committing to the movement versus waiting for perfect conditions.

Market orders are simple. They remove hesitation. They are often appropriate for long-term investors who are not trying to time short-term price changes.

Limit orders feel more controlled, but they can create delays. Sometimes the price never reaches your target, and you miss the opportunity entirely.

Neither is inherently right or wrong. What matters is intent. Long-term investing is not choreography that requires perfect timing. It is consistency.

Most dancers are better served by simplicity than by precision.

Buy-and-Hold Discipline

Buy-and-hold means purchasing investments with the intention of keeping them for long periods, often years or decades. It does not mean ignoring your portfolio forever. It means resisting the urge to constantly change it based on headlines, fear, or short-term performance.

This is where many athletes struggle.

You are trained to adjust quickly. To respond to feedback. To fix mistakes immediately. In investing, that instinct can backfire.

Markets move constantly. Ups and downs are normal. Volatility does not mean something is broken. It means movement is happening.

Selling every time discomfort appears is like quitting a piece because it feels awkward after the first rehearsal. You never give the work time to develop.

Buy-and-hold discipline allows compounding to work. Compounding requires time, not activity. The less you interfere, the more powerful it becomes.

Doing less is often the hardest skill to learn.

Avoiding Emotional Decisions

Emotions are not the enemy. They are information. The problem arises when emotions drive decisions instead of awareness.

Common emotional triggers include:

- Fear during market drops
- Excitement during rapid gains
- Comparison with others
- Regret over missed opportunities

Dancers know this feeling well. One bad rehearsal can shake confidence. One strong performance can inflate it. Neither should redefine the entire process.

Financially, emotional decisions often show up as:

- Panic selling
- Chasing hot investments
- Abandoning a plan mid-cycle
- Constant second-guessing

These actions rarely improve outcomes. They usually lock in mistakes.

Systems protect you from yourself. Automated contributions, clear allocation targets, and written plans reduce the need to decide in the heat of the moment.

You do not rise to the level of your motivation. You fall to the level of your systems.

Trusting the Process When Results Are Invisible

One of the hardest parts of investing is that progress is not always visible.

You can practice for months without noticeable improvement. You can invest for years before compounding feels meaningful. That does not mean the work is wasted.

Early stages are about foundation. Later stages reveal the payoff.

Dancers understand delayed rewards better than most people. You trained long before the audience ever saw the result. Investing follows that same arc.

Trust is not blind. It is earned through understanding and consistency.

Coach's Perspective

A coach would keep this simple.

They would say:

- Do the work
- Stick to the plan
- Do not panic after one bad day
- Repetition beats intensity
- Finish what you start

Great outcomes come from boring consistency.

Game Situations and Decision Points

You open an account but hesitate to fund it. Do you wait for confidence or build it through action?

Markets drop. Do you abandon your strategy or continue contributing?

You hear about a new investment everyone is excited about. Do you chase it or stay grounded?

These moments define long-term results far more than investment selection.

Common Performer Mistakes and Financial Parallels

Dancers often overcorrect after small mistakes. Financially, this shows up as frequent trading.

Dancers compare themselves constantly. Financially, this leads to chasing someone else's returns.

Dancers lose patience when progress feels slow. Financially, this results in abandoning compounding too early.

The discipline that built your technique can build your wealth, if you let it.

Winning the Long Career

Careers are not defined by one performance. Wealth is not defined by one investment.

Buying, holding, and trusting the process is how progress compounds quietly in the background while you focus on living your life.

When your financial system is steady, you gain creative freedom. You take roles because they matter, not because you are desperate. You move with confidence because your foundation is secure.

That is real control.

Athlete Takeaways

- Open the right accounts and fund them consistently.
- Simplicity beats precision for long-term investing.
- Buy-and-hold requires patience, not perfection.
- Systems protect you from emotional decisions.
- Trust the process the same way you trusted your training.

Chapter 17: Rebalancing and Career Transitions

In dance, no career stays static. Training changes. Roles evolve. Bodies age. Priorities shift. What worked during one phase of your career may not serve you in the next, and adjusting does not mean you failed. It means you are paying attention.

Investing works the same way.

Rebalancing is not about chasing performance or fixing mistakes. It is about maintaining alignment as conditions change. Career transitions, income swings, and life events naturally pull your financial plan out of balance. Rebalancing is how you bring it back into form without overreacting.

This chapter is about awareness, restraint, and thoughtful adjustment.

How Often to Review Investments

Reviewing your investments does not mean constantly changing them.

Many performers confuse *reviewing* with *tinkering*. Reviewing is observation. Tinkering is interference. One builds clarity. The other builds anxiety.

For most people, reviewing investments once or twice per year is enough. That cadence allows you to:

- Check whether your allocation still matches your goals

- Confirm contributions are happening as planned
- Notice drift without panicking

In dance terms, this is like a seasonal assessment, not a daily self-critique. You do not rewrite choreography every rehearsal. You check alignment, spacing, and timing, then keep moving.

Constant monitoring invites emotional decisions. Infrequent review invites neglect. Balance sits in the middle.

What Rebalancing Actually Means

Rebalancing is the act of bringing your portfolio back to its intended structure.

Over time, different investments grow at different rates. Stocks may rise faster than bonds. Certain sectors may surge. Without intervention, your portfolio slowly becomes more aggressive or more conservative than you intended.

Rebalancing does not judge which investment is "good" or "bad." It simply restores proportions.

If your plan calls for balance and growth has tilted you toward risk, rebalancing trims excess and redistributes. If markets decline and safety dominates, rebalancing gently reintroduces growth.

This is maintenance, not correction.

In dance, this is posture. You constantly make small adjustments to stay centered. You do not wait until you fall to respond.

Common Rebalancing Strategies

There are several disciplined ways to rebalance. The best one is the one you can follow consistently.

Calendar-based rebalancing

You rebalance on a fixed schedule, such as once per year. Simple. Predictable. Emotion-free.

Threshold-based rebalancing

You rebalance only when allocations drift beyond set ranges. This requires more monitoring but less frequent action.

Contribution-based rebalancing

Instead of selling investments, you direct new contributions toward underweighted areas. This is often the least disruptive approach.

Each method works when applied consistently. None work if used reactively.

The goal is not to optimize returns. The goal is to control risk and stay aligned with your life.

Income Changes and Portfolio Updates

Performers experience income changes more frequently than most professions. Contracts end. Tours vary. Teaching, choreography, and freelance work fluctuate. That reality makes flexibility essential.

When income changes, rebalancing may be appropriate, but not always immediately.

Key questions to ask:

- Is this change temporary or structural?
- Does it affect my ability to save or invest consistently?
- Does it change my time horizon or risk tolerance?

A short-term income dip does not require a complete financial overhaul. Panic adjustments often cause more harm than patience.

However, long-term changes may require thoughtful updates. Shifting from performing to teaching, freelancing to salaried work, or active income to reduced workload can all justify gradual portfolio adjustments.

Career transitions are not emergencies. They are phases.

Avoiding Over-Adjustment

One of the most common mistakes performers make financially is over-adjusting.

Over-adjustment looks like:

- Changing strategy after every market swing
- Constantly reallocating based on recent performance
- Abandoning long-term plans during temporary discomfort

This behavior often comes from a desire to stay in control. Ironically, it creates instability.

In dance, over-adjustment disrupts flow. You stop trusting your body and start micromanaging every movement. The result is tension, not improvement.

Financially, the same principle applies. Too much intervention breaks compounding and increases stress.

Discipline is not rigidity. It is restraint.

Transitions Without Losing Structure

Career transitions test financial systems. Touring ends. Schedules change. Identity shifts. Structure disappears if you do not replace it intentionally.

Rebalancing during transitions should be gradual and deliberate. Small adjustments preserve momentum. Sudden shifts often create regret.

Instead of asking, "What should I change right now?" ask:

- "What still works?"
- "What needs time?"
- "What can I adjust without urgency?"

This mindset keeps you grounded.

Coach's Perspective

A coach would likely say:

- Do not fix what is not broken
- Make adjustments, not excuses
- Stay patient through transitions
- Trust your preparation
- Do not chase last night's performance

Rebalancing is not reactive. It is disciplined maintenance.

Game Situations and Decision Points

Your portfolio has grown, but now feels riskier than before. Do you rebalance calmly or wait for fear to force action?

Your income changes temporarily. Do you overhaul your plan or ride out the transition?

Markets fluctuate. Do you adjust everything or stay within your system?

These moments define long-term outcomes more than market direction.

Common Performer Mistakes and Financial Parallels

Performers often chase momentum. Financially, that becomes performance chasing.

Performers overanalyze transitions. Financially, that leads to unnecessary changes.

Performers struggle with patience during uncertainty. Financially, that causes poor timing.

The same discipline that sustained your career can sustain your finances.

Winning the Long Career

Longevity requires adjustment without panic.

Rebalancing allows your financial life to evolve without losing direction. It protects you from extremes and keeps your system aligned as your career unfolds.

Success is not staying the same. It is adapting with intention.

Athlete Takeaways

- Review regularly, but do not obsess.
- Rebalance to restore alignment, not chase returns.
- Let income transitions settle before making big changes.
- Avoid over-adjustment during emotional moments.
- Maintain structure while allowing your career to evolve.

Chapter 18: The Mental Side of Money

Money decisions are rarely just about numbers. They are about emotion, identity, and pressure. For dancers, this mental layer is often more challenging than the technical side of finances. You were trained to pursue perfection, compare yourself to others, and perform under scrutiny. Those same traits that helped you succeed artistically can quietly undermine your financial confidence if they are not managed intentionally.

This chapter is about the internal work. The part no one sees. The mental discipline required to handle money with the same composure you learned to bring to rehearsal, performance, and transition.

Pressure, Comparison, and Perfectionism

Dance culture is built on comparison.

Mirrors.

Auditions.

Casting lists.

Reviews.

Social media.

You are constantly exposed to who got the role, who advanced faster, who looks stronger, who seems more successful. Over time, comparison becomes background noise, and perfectionism feels normal.

Money amplifies this dynamic.

You compare salaries, lifestyles, apartments, vacations, and perceived success. You wonder if you are behind. You question whether you should be doing more, earning more, investing more, or living differently. Pressure builds quietly, and perfectionism turns financial decisions into emotional tests.

Perfectionism shows up financially as:

- Waiting to act until everything feels "just right"
- Avoiding decisions out of fear of making the wrong one
- Constantly second-guessing progress
- Feeling behind even when you are doing fine

Money does not reward perfection. It rewards consistency. Just like dance, progress comes from showing up repeatedly, not from flawless execution.

Managing Uncertainty and Downtime

Downtime is part of a dancer's life.

Contracts end.

Seasons pause.

Injuries happen.

Auditions slow.

Even successful careers include gaps, and those gaps test both emotional resilience and financial confidence.

Uncertainty creates mental noise:

- Should I spend less right now?
- Should I hold off on investing?
- Should I change everything?
- What if this lasts longer than I expect?

The instinct is often to react. To either freeze completely or abandon discipline out of stress.

The healthier response is to separate uncertainty from panic.

Downtime does not mean failure.

It does not mean your system is broken.

It does not mean you need to start over.

Financial systems are built to absorb pauses when they are designed intentionally. Emergency funds, flexible budgets, and conservative assumptions exist for this reason. They are not signs of pessimism. They are signs of maturity.

Managing uncertainty is about staying steady when circumstances fluctuate.

Building Systems for Discipline

Motivation is unreliable.

Discipline is durable.

Most people assume financial success comes from willpower. It does not. It comes from systems that reduce decision fatigue and remove emotion from routine actions.

Effective systems include:

- Automatic savings contributions
- Scheduled bill payments
- Clear account separation
- Simple, repeatable investment plans

These systems do not require constant attention. They work quietly in the background, allowing you to focus on your career and life without obsessing over money.

In dance terms, this is muscle memory. You do not consciously think through every movement on stage. You trained the system so your body could perform under pressure.

Financial systems work the same way. They protect you when stress, fatigue, or distraction would otherwise lead to poor decisions.

Staying Grounded Through Change

Change is inevitable.

Career shifts.

Location changes.

Income changes.

Identity changes.

What destabilizes people is not change itself. It is losing internal reference points during change.

Staying grounded financially means maintaining a few anchors:

- Knowing your basic numbers
- Keeping routines around saving and spending
- Revisiting long-term goals during transitions
- Avoiding impulsive changes based on fear or comparison

Grounding does not mean rigidity. It means awareness.

You are allowed to adjust.

You are allowed to evolve.

You are allowed to change direction.

What matters is doing so intentionally, not emotionally.

Coach's Perspective

If a coach addressed the mental side of money, the message would feel familiar:

- Control what you can control
- Do not compare your process to someone else's outcome
- Stay patient during uncertainty
- Trust your training
- Focus on fundamentals when pressure rises

Mental discipline is not about eliminating emotion. It is about not letting emotion drive decisions.

Game Situations and Decision Points

You see peers posting lifestyles that seem far beyond yours. Do you question your entire plan or refocus on your own process?

You experience downtime. Do you abandon systems or rely on them to carry you through?

You feel behind. Do you rush decisions or recommit to consistency?

These moments define financial outcomes more than income ever will.

Common Performer Mistakes and Financial Parallels

Dancers chase perfection. Financially, that leads to paralysis.

Dancers compare relentlessly. Financially, that leads to dissatisfaction.

Dancers push through exhaustion. Financially, that leads to burnout and poor choices.

Awareness turns these tendencies into strengths instead of liabilities.

Winning the Long Career

Longevity in dance requires emotional regulation, patience, and adaptability. Money demands the same skills.

You do not need to be fearless.

You do not need to be perfect.

You do not need to have it all figured out.

You need to stay grounded, disciplined, and consistent through change.

That is how careers last.

That is how finances grow.

That is how confidence is built quietly over time.

Athlete Takeaways

- Comparison is noise. Stay focused on your own process.
- Perfectionism delays progress. Consistency builds it.
- Systems protect you when motivation fades.
- Downtime tests discipline, not worth.
- Staying grounded through change is a skill you already have.

Part V: Life Beyond the Stage

Every dance career eventually reaches a turning point.

It might come through injury, burnout, changing priorities, or simply time. Sometimes it arrives quietly. Other times it shows up all at once. However it happens, life beyond the stage is not a loss of identity or a failure of talent. It is a natural transition in a career built on physical demand, discipline, and constant evaluation.

This part of the book is about navigating that transition with clarity instead of fear.

When the Structure Changes

Dance provides structure for nearly everything. Rehearsal schedules. Performance seasons. Contracts. Feedback loops. When that structure fades or shifts, many dancers feel unmoored.

Financial stress often appears at the same time. Income becomes inconsistent. Benefits disappear. Long-term planning feels unclear. These challenges are not personal shortcomings. They are the result of moving from a system that once managed many details for you into one where you must create your own structure.

Understanding your money during this phase gives you back control when external systems change.

Identity Beyond Performance

For many dancers, identity is closely tied to performing.

When performance slows or stops, the question naturally arises: who am I without this?

That question can affect financial decisions. Some dancers rush into new paths for security. Others delay decisions out of uncertainty. Both reactions are understandable. Neither has to define the outcome.

Financial stability during transition creates breathing room. It allows you to explore who you are becoming without panic shaping every choice.

Redefining Success

Success after dance looks different for everyone.

For some, it means predictable income.

For others, flexibility or time.

For others, impact, teaching, or creative freedom.

The key is recognizing that success is no longer measured by roles, applause, or external validation. It is measured by alignment between your values and how you live.

Money should support that alignment, not replace one form of pressure with another.

Skills That Still Matter

Dancers often underestimate how valuable their skills remain beyond the stage.

Discipline.

Coachability.

Attention to detail.

Resilience.

Comfort with repetition and feedback.

These qualities transfer directly into careers, finances, and long-term planning. You are not starting from scratch. You are applying familiar habits in a new context.

The same consistency that built technique can build financial stability over time.

Stability as Freedom

Stability does not limit creativity. It protects it.

When your financial foundation is organized, you gain options. You can pursue education, explore new careers, or stay connected to dance on your own terms. You are less likely to accept misaligned opportunities out of fear.

Financial organization creates space for thoughtful choices instead of reactive ones.

Moving Forward Without Erasing the Past

Honoring your dance career does not require living in it forever.

Your training mattered.

Your sacrifices mattered.

Your experience still matters.

Life beyond the stage is not about abandoning your past. It is about integrating it into a broader identity that continues to evolve.

Closing Perspective

You spent years learning balance, control, and precision. Those same principles apply offstage.

When the routine changes, the fundamentals still hold.

Life beyond the stage is not an ending.

It is a new movement.

Handled with intention, it can be just as purposeful and fulfilling as the one that came before.

Chapter 19: Taxes and Where You Place Your Earnings

Taxes are not the most exciting part of money, but they are one of the most powerful.

Many dancers work hard to earn income, yet give little thought to where that income lives once it arrives. The result is often higher taxes, lost opportunities, and unnecessary stress later. This chapter is about understanding how taxes actually work and how smart placement of your earnings can protect more of what you work so hard to earn.

In dance terms, this is about spacing and positioning. The same movement performed in the wrong place can throw off the entire routine. Money works the same way.

Why Taxes Feel Confusing to Performers

Most dancers do not grow up with predictable paychecks.

Income may come from contracts, gigs, teaching, choreography, touring, or freelance work. Some income is taxed automatically. Some is not. Some arrives with paperwork. Some does not.

Without guidance, taxes feel reactive. You earn, you spend, and then you hope tax season is manageable.

That approach creates surprises.

Taxes are not something you deal with once a year. They are something you manage year-round through how and where you earn, save, and invest.

Taxable vs Tax-Advantaged Accounts

Where your money sits matters as much as how much you earn.

Taxable accounts are accounts with no special tax treatment.

Examples include:

- Checking and savings accounts
- Brokerage accounts
- Most side business income accounts

In taxable accounts, interest, dividends, and investment gains can be taxed along the way.

Tax-advantaged accounts are designed to encourage long-term saving by offering tax benefits.

Examples include:

- Retirement accounts
- Certain employer-sponsored plans

These accounts are governed by rules, but they offer meaningful advantages if used correctly.

In dance terms, taxable accounts are like rehearsing in an open studio. You have flexibility, but little protection. Tax-advantaged accounts are like working within a structured program. There are rules, but the environment supports long-term performance.

Tax-Deferred vs Tax-Free Growth

Not all tax advantages work the same way.

Tax-deferred growth means you delay taxes until later.

You typically receive a tax break today, but pay taxes when you withdraw the money in the future.

This can be powerful if your income is higher now than you expect it to be later.

Tax-free growth means you pay taxes upfront, but future growth and withdrawals may be tax-free if rules are followed.

This provides clarity and flexibility later, especially when income becomes unpredictable or fixed.

In dance terms, tax-deferred growth is like pushing through intense training now and resting later. Tax-free growth is like doing the work early so future performances feel lighter.

Neither is universally better. The right choice depends on income, career stage, and long-term goals.

Asset Location Basics

Asset location is different from asset allocation.

Allocation is what you invest in.

Location is where those investments live.

Some types of investments generate more taxable income than others. Placing them in the right type of account can reduce the taxes you owe over time.

For example:

- Investments that generate frequent income are often more tax-efficient inside tax-advantaged accounts
- Investments focused on long-term growth may work better in certain taxable environments

The goal is not complexity. The goal is alignment.

In dance, you would not place the most demanding sequence at the end of a routine without planning for it. Asset location is that same planning applied to money.

Common Tax Mistakes Dancers Make

Many tax mistakes are not dramatic. They are quiet and repeated.

Common issues include:

- Not setting aside money for taxes from freelance income
- Treating all accounts as interchangeable
- Ignoring tax impact when investing
- Waiting until tax season to think about planning
- Assuming higher income automatically means better outcomes

These mistakes compound over time, just like small technical errors repeated across rehearsals.

Taxes punish disorganization more than low income.

Why Proactive Planning Matters

Tax planning is not about avoiding taxes.

It is about understanding the rules and working within them.

Proactive planning helps you:

- Keep more of what you earn
- Reduce surprises
- Create flexibility during career transitions
- Make confident long-term decisions

For dancers with variable income, planning is even more important. Good years can help support leaner seasons, but only if taxes are handled intentionally.

Coach's Perspective

If a coach were talking about taxes, the message would be simple.
Do not wait until performance day to think about preparation.
Understand the rules before you step on stage.
Details matter even when they are boring.
Clean execution prevents deductions you cannot recover from.
Taxes are part of the routine whether you like them or not.

Game Situations and Decision Points

You earn freelance income.
Do you set aside money immediately, or hope it works out later?
You open a new investment account.
Do you consider tax treatment, or only potential returns?
You experience a strong earning year.
Do you plan strategically, or let taxes erase the momentum?
Each decision shapes what stays with you long-term.

Common Performer Mistakes and Financial Parallels

Performers focus on gross pay.
Financially, that ignores what you actually keep.
Performers delay administrative work.
Financially, that leads to penalties and stress.
Performers chase opportunity without structure.
Financially, that leads to inefficiency.
The same discipline that protects performance protects earnings.

Winning the Long Game

A long career requires planning beyond the next performance.

Taxes reward preparation, patience, and structure. You do not need to master every rule. You need to understand enough to place your earnings thoughtfully and ask for help when needed.

Money kept through smart planning compounds just like skill built through consistent practice.

Athlete Takeaways

- Where your money lives matters as much as how much you earn
- Tax-advantaged accounts reward long-term discipline
- Tax-deferred and tax-free growth serve different stages of a career
- Asset location is about smart placement, not complexity
- Clean financial technique prevents costly deductions over time

Chapter 20: Retirement Accounts and Financial Independence

For many dancers, retirement feels abstract.

You train your body to perform now. Your career often rewards youth, flexibility, and availability. Thinking decades ahead can feel disconnected from the reality of auditions, contracts, rehearsals, and recovery. Yet financial independence is built the same way a long-performing body is built. Slowly. Intentionally. With respect for limits and recovery.

Retirement accounts are not about stopping work. They are about gaining control.

They give you options. Options change everything.

Why Retirement Feels So Distant to Performers

Most dancers do not experience linear careers.

Income may rise and fall. Benefits may come and go. Some years feel stable. Others feel uncertain. Because of that, retirement planning often gets postponed until things feel "settled."

The problem is that compounding rewards early action more than perfect timing.

Retirement accounts are not about predicting your future. They are about preparing for it without needing to guess every detail.

In dance terms, this is cross-training. You may not need it for tonight's show, but without it, longevity suffers.

Employer Plans and Pensions

Some dancers encounter employer-sponsored plans through schools, universities, companies, or secondary careers.

These plans may include:

- Employer retirement plans with matching contributions
- Pension-style benefits in certain institutions

If an employer offers a match, it is part of your compensation. Not using it is like skipping paid rehearsal time.

Employer plans offer:

- Automatic contributions
- Potential matching dollars
- Tax advantages
- Simplicity

Even small contributions matter. What feels insignificant now compounds into meaningful support later.

If your employment situation changes frequently, consistency matters more than contribution size. Keeping the habit alive matters more than chasing perfection.

Traditional and Roth IRAs

Individual Retirement Accounts exist for people without consistent employer plans and for those who want additional flexibility.

There are two common types.

Traditional IRAs

Contributions may reduce taxable income now. Taxes are paid later when money is withdrawn.

This can be helpful in higher-income years when current tax relief matters.

Roth IRAs

Contributions are made with after-tax money. Growth and qualified withdrawals can be tax-free later.

This can be powerful for performers whose income fluctuates and who value future flexibility.

In dance terms, a Traditional IRA is like conserving energy now and pushing later. A Roth IRA is like doing the hard work early so later movement feels lighter.

Neither is better in all cases. Many performers benefit from a combination over time.

Contribution Rules and Consistency

Retirement accounts come with rules.

There are limits on how much you can contribute each year. There are guidelines for eligibility. There are penalties for breaking withdrawal rules.

These rules are not obstacles. They are structure.

Structure protects discipline when motivation fades.

Contributing regularly matters more than contributing aggressively. Small, consistent deposits outperform large, inconsistent efforts.

Just like daily technique class beats occasional marathon rehearsals, consistency compounds quietly.

Withdrawal Rules and Respecting the Timeline

Retirement accounts are designed for long-term use.

Withdrawing money early may trigger taxes and penalties. These consequences exist to protect the long-term purpose of the account.

For dancers, respecting these boundaries is critical. Retirement accounts are not emergency funds. They are not checking accounts. They are not solutions for short-term gaps.

Using the right account for the right purpose prevents cascading mistakes.

In performance terms, this is pacing. You do not expend everything in the opening sequence and expect to finish strong.

Retirement Income Basics

Retirement income does not arrive as a single event.

It is a process.

Income in later life may come from:

- Retirement account withdrawals
- Employer benefits or pensions
- Personal savings
- Part-time work or teaching
- Other long-term assets

Financial independence is not about never working again. It is about choosing how and when you work without financial pressure forcing decisions.

For performers, this often means transitioning roles rather than stopping entirely.

Teaching. Coaching. Directing. Creating. Consulting.

Retirement accounts support those transitions by reducing urgency.

Why Financial Independence Matters More Than a Number

Many people define retirement by an age or a dollar amount.

For dancers, a better definition is control.

Can you say no to work that compromises your health?

Can you take time to recover without panic?

Can you transition careers without starting over financially?

Financial independence provides freedom of movement. That freedom protects your body, your creativity, and your identity.

Coach's Perspective

If a coach talked about retirement planning, it would sound familiar.

Start early.

Be consistent.

Respect recovery and limits.

Do not wait until you are injured to care about longevity.

You do not train for one performance. You train for a career.

Retirement accounts are part of that training.

Game Situations and Decision Points

You have a good earning year.

Do you increase lifestyle spending or increase long-term contributions?

You leave a job with a retirement plan.

Do you ignore the account or intentionally move it forward?

You hesitate to start because contributions feel small.

Do you wait for perfect conditions or start building now?

These choices compound quietly.

Common Performer Mistakes and Financial Parallels

Performers delay planning.

Financially, that sacrifices compounding.

Performers rely on future opportunities.

Financially, that creates pressure later.

Performers avoid rules.

Financially, that leads to penalties and lost benefits.

The same discipline that protects technique protects finances.

Winning the Long Game

A long-performing career requires planning beyond the next contract.

Retirement accounts are not exciting, but they are powerful. They reward patience. They protect options. They reduce stress when transitions arrive.

Financial independence is not about quitting. It is about choosing.

That choice is earned through consistent preparation, not sudden success.

Athlete Takeaways

- Retirement accounts are about control, not stopping work
- Employer matches are earned compensation, not optional
- Traditional and Roth accounts serve different career stages
- Consistency beats contribution size
- Financial independence protects your ability to choose your next move

Chapter 21: Housing and Major Financial Decisions

Major financial decisions shape a dancer's life far beyond the numbers on paper.

Where you live. How you commute. What you finance. These choices affect flexibility, recovery, stress, and opportunity. Unlike a single performance, these decisions linger. They either support your career and well-being, or they quietly drain energy over time.

For dancers, housing and large purchases are not lifestyle trophies. They are structural choices that either protect longevity or compromise it.

Renting vs Buying: Stability Versus Flexibility

The rent-versus-buy debate is often framed as a competition. In reality, it is a timing decision.

Renting offers flexibility.

You can relocate for contracts, tours, auditions, or new opportunities. Maintenance is not your responsibility. Upfront costs are lower. Cash flow is easier to manage when income fluctuates.

In dance terms, renting is like staying light on your feet. You can adjust direction quickly without carrying unnecessary weight.

Buying offers stability and long-term potential.

You build equity. Monthly payments may eventually stabilize. You gain control over your living environment.

Buying is like committing to a long-term role. When the timing fits, it can be grounding. When it does not, it can limit movement.

There is no universal right answer. The decision depends on:

- Income stability
- Career stage
- Geographic consistency
- Cash reserves
- Willingness to handle responsibility

Buying too early is like locking into choreography your body is not ready to sustain. It may look impressive, but execution suffers.

The Hidden Costs of Homeownership

Many performers underestimate the true cost of owning a home.

Ownership includes:

- Maintenance and repairs
- Property taxes
- Insurance
- Utilities
- Unexpected expenses
- Reduced mobility

These costs do not pause during injuries, slow seasons, or career transitions.

In dance terms, this is ignoring recovery and assuming your body will always cooperate. When something goes wrong, the margin for error disappears.

Homeownership works best when:

- Cash flow is predictable
- Emergency reserves are solid

- Location fits long-term plans
- Stress does not compromise performance

Owning a home should support your life, not anchor you to pressure.

Mortgages and Down Payments

A mortgage is leverage. It allows you to control a large asset with a smaller upfront commitment.

Leverage amplifies outcomes. That can work in your favor or against you.

Down payments matter because they:

- Reduce monthly obligations
- Lower interest costs
- Increase flexibility

Stretching too far because you "qualify" is a common mistake. Approval is not the same as affordability.

In dance terms, this is dancing at maximum intensity without regard for endurance. You may last for a while, but sustainability suffers.

A smart mortgage:

- Fits comfortably within cash flow
- Allows continued saving and investing
- Does not rely on future income increases to survive

You should still be able to breathe after the purchase.

Cars, Leases, and Financing Traps

Transportation is a necessity. The mistake is turning necessity into excess.

Cars depreciate. They lose value over time. Financing decisions around vehicles often drain more wealth than almost any other category.

Common traps include:

- Long-term loans on depreciating assets
- Leasing without understanding mileage or wear limits
- Choosing payments based on monthly comfort instead of total cost

Leases can work in specific situations, but they often prioritize convenience over efficiency. Frequent vehicle changes may feel flexible but quietly consume cash flow.

In performance terms, this is replacing shoes too often for aesthetic reasons rather than function. It looks good, but it adds unnecessary cost.

A reliable, affordable vehicle supports your career without becoming a financial distraction.

Financing and Emotional Decision-Making

Large purchases often trigger emotion.

You feel established. You feel behind. You want to reward effort. You compare yourself to peers. These feelings are real, but they are dangerous guides.

Major financial decisions should be made when emotions are calm.

Ask:

- Does this increase or reduce flexibility?
- What happens if income drops?
- What does this cost me long-term, not just monthly?
- Does this support my career, health, and goals?

Emotion fades. Payments remain.

Planning Major Purchases Intentionally

Major purchases should be planned, not reacted to.

Planning includes:

- Saving intentionally for down payments
- Stress-testing decisions against income changes
- Understanding total cost, not just monthly payment
- Timing purchases to match career phases

In dance terms, this is rehearsal. You do not debut choreography without preparation. Financial commitments deserve the same respect.

Planning creates confidence. Confidence prevents regret.

Coach's Perspective

If a coach were advising on major financial decisions, the guidance would be familiar.

Know your body.

Know your limits.

Do not sacrifice longevity for short-term comfort.

Choose sustainability over flash.

Think beyond the next performance.

Housing and large purchases are part of your career strategy, not rewards for surviving another season.

Game Situations and Decision Points

You feel pressure to buy because others are buying.

Do you follow the crowd or honor your timing?

You qualify for more than you expected.

Do you take the maximum or choose control?

Your income increases temporarily.

Do you lock in higher fixed costs or protect flexibility?

The right decision often feels boring. Boring is usually sustainable.

Common Performer Mistakes and Financial Parallels

Performers chase stability too early.

Financially, that limits mobility.

Performers underestimate downtime.

Financially, that leads to stress during slow periods.

Performers reward effort with expensive commitments.

Financially, that erodes long-term options.

The same patience that builds technique builds security.

Winning the Long Game

Housing and major purchases should serve your life, not define it.

Financial independence is supported by choices that preserve movement, protect cash flow, and reduce stress. These decisions rarely impress others, but they quietly support careers that last.

You do not need to own everything. You need to control your options.

That is what smart decisions deliver.

Athlete Takeaways

- Renting preserves flexibility; buying requires stability
- Approval does not equal affordability
- Cars should support life, not drain momentum
- Plan major purchases like choreography, not improvisation
- Sustainability beats status every time

Chapter 22: Your Career Is a Portfolio

In dance, no single performance defines you.

A career is built across seasons, companies, styles, injuries, recoveries, and reinventions. Some years are full. Others are quiet. Some opportunities pay well but cost creatively. Others feed the soul but strain the budget. Dancers learn early that longevity depends on adaptability, not perfection.

Your career works the same way financially.

Most people think of a career as one job, one paycheck, one title. That mindset is limiting, especially for dancers. A smarter way to think about your work is as a **portfolio**. Different income sources. Different risks. Different timelines. All working together to support stability, growth, and opportunity.

When you see your career as a portfolio, you stop chasing single outcomes and start building something resilient.

Salary vs Total Compensation

Many performers focus only on pay rate.

Hourly wage. Weekly contract. Per-show rate.

That matters, but it is not the full picture.

Total compensation includes everything attached to the work, not just cash:

- Health insurance or benefits

- Retirement contributions
- Housing stipends or per diems
- Paid rehearsal time
- Schedule stability
- Networking value
- Career credibility

A lower-paying role with benefits and consistency may outperform a higher-paying gig that offers no protection and unpredictable hours.

In dance terms, this is choosing a role based not just on applause, but on how it fits your body, schedule, and future.

Smart dancers ask:

- What does this role give me beyond money?
- What does it cost me in flexibility, energy, or risk?
- How does this fit into my larger career arc?

Money is one metric. Sustainability is the goal.

Contract Work and Freelance Income

Many dancers live in a freelance reality.

Short-term contracts. Teaching gigs. Choreography projects. Guest appearances. Touring work. Each opportunity may look separate, but financially, they form a single system.

Freelance income creates freedom. It also creates responsibility.

With contract work:

- Income is irregular
- Benefits are often missing
- Taxes are your responsibility
- Planning matters more than ever

In dance terms, freelancing is like performing across multiple companies without a full-time home base. It builds range and exposure, but it requires discipline behind the scenes.

Key principles for managing freelance income:

- Save during high-income months
- Plan for dry spells
- Separate business and personal finances
- Track income consistently

The mistake is spending like income is guaranteed when it is not.

Freelancers who succeed financially treat unpredictability as a known variable, not a surprise.

Negotiation Basics for Performers

Negotiation often feels uncomfortable for dancers.

You are taught to be grateful. To not make waves. To accept what is offered. But negotiation is not arrogance. It is communication.

Negotiation does not mean demanding more than you deserve. It means understanding your value and advocating for fairness.

You can negotiate:

- Pay rates
- Housing support
- Scheduling flexibility
- Travel reimbursement
- Contract length
- Payment timing

In performance terms, negotiation is knowing your worth without ego. You would not accept choreography that injures you long-term. Financial harm deserves the same boundary.

Effective negotiation starts with preparation:

- Know standard rates
- Understand what you need to say yes
- Be clear about priorities
- Stay professional and calm

Sometimes the answer will still be no. That is information, not failure.
Strong negotiators protect relationships while protecting themselves.

Side Income and Entrepreneurship

Many dancers develop side income out of necessity.
Teaching. Coaching. Fitness training. Choreography. Content creation. Brand partnerships. Small businesses. Creative projects.
Side income is not a sign you failed as a performer. It is often a sign you are adapting.
Entrepreneurship allows dancers to:

- Reduce reliance on a single income source
- Monetize expertise
- Build skills beyond performance
- Create long-term options

In dance terms, this is cross-training. It does not replace your main discipline. It supports it.
That said, side income should be intentional.
Questions to ask:

- Does this drain or support my energy?
- Is it scalable or time-bound?
- Does it align with my values and long-term goals?
- Am I tracking income and expenses properly?

Not every opportunity deserves a yes. Burnout is real.

The goal is not to hustle endlessly. The goal is to build a career that holds up over time.

Diversifying Your Career Portfolio

Just like investing, diversification reduces risk.

Relying on one company, one contract, or one skill creates vulnerability. Spreading effort across complementary roles builds stability.

A balanced career portfolio may include:

- Performance income
- Teaching or coaching
- Creative projects
- Administrative or production roles
- Education or certifications
- Entrepreneurial ventures

Each piece plays a role.

In dance terms, this is being versatile without losing identity. You do not abandon technique. You expand application.

Diversification protects you when injuries happen, contracts end, or industries shift.

Coach's Perspective

If a coach were advising you on your career as a portfolio, the message would be direct.

Know your strengths.

Do not rely on one move.

Protect your body and your future.

Prepare for transitions before you need them.

Think long-term.

Careers are not won in one season. They are sustained through smart planning and adaptability.

Game Situations and Decision Points

You are offered a higher-paying gig with no benefits.

Do you evaluate total compensation or chase the number?

You want to negotiate but fear losing the role.

Do you stay silent or advocate professionally?

You are exhausted but see another side opportunity.

Do you add income or protect capacity?

Each choice shapes the portfolio.

Common Performer Mistakes and Financial Parallels

Performers focus only on pay rate.

Financially, that ignores risk and sustainability.

Performers avoid negotiation.

Financially, that leads to chronic underpayment.

Performers say yes to everything.

Financially, that leads to burnout and poor decisions.

Discipline offstage matters as much as discipline onstage.

Winning the Long Game

Careers evolve. Bodies change. Interests shift. Income patterns fluctuate.

The dancers who succeed long-term are not the ones who cling to one identity. They are the ones who build layered, flexible careers that adapt without panic.

Seeing your career as a portfolio gives you control.

You stop reacting.

You start choosing.

You build options.

That is financial independence in motion.

Athlete Takeaways

- Your career is a portfolio, not a single role
- Total compensation matters more than pay rate alone
- Freelance income requires planning, not hope
- Negotiation is professionalism, not ego
- Side income should support longevity, not burn you out

Chapter 23: Estate Planning Basics Everyone Needs

Estate planning sounds like something you deal with later. Much later. After a long career. After big money. After everything feels settled.

That mindset leaves a lot of dancers exposed.

Estate planning is not about wealth. It is about **control**. It answers one simple question: *If something happens to you, who makes decisions, and what happens next?* Without answers, the system decides for you. Courts. State laws. Strangers. Default rules that do not know your values, relationships, or intentions.

In dance terms, estate planning is not a grand finale. It is basic technique. Quiet, disciplined work that prevents chaos when something unexpected happens.

You do not plan because you expect something bad. You plan because careers, bodies, and life are unpredictable.

Why Estate Planning Matters for Performers

Dancers face unique realities.

Careers can be short.

Income can be irregular.

Health risks are real.

Many dancers live far from family.

Relationships and support systems often look nontraditional.

Without proper planning, even small estates become complicated. Accounts can get frozen. Loved ones can be locked out of decisions. Medical wishes can be ignored. Financial stress piles onto emotional stress.

Estate planning is not about death. It is about **protection while you are alive** and clarity if you are not able to speak for yourself.

Wills: Setting the Baseline

A will is the foundation of any estate plan.

It outlines:

- Who receives your assets
- Who manages your estate
- Who handles responsibilities if you have dependents
- How personal property is distributed

Without a will, state law decides everything. That process is slow, public, and often misaligned with what you would want.

For dancers, a will helps:

- Protect family members or chosen family
- Avoid confusion among parents, partners, or siblings
- Clarify intentions around personal items, savings, and accounts
- Name someone you trust to handle logistics

In performance terms, a will is choreography on paper. Without it, everyone improvises under pressure.

A simple will is better than no will. It can always be updated as life changes.

Trusts: When and Why They Matter

Trusts are often misunderstood.

They are not only for the wealthy. They are tools for control, efficiency, and privacy.

A trust allows assets to be managed and distributed according to rules you set. It can help:

- Avoid probate
- Provide structure for beneficiaries
- Manage assets if someone is not ready to handle them
- Protect privacy
- Plan for incapacity

Not every dancer needs a trust immediately. But some situations make trusts more useful:

- Significant savings or investments
- Property ownership
- Blended families
- Dependents with special needs
- Desire for privacy or control

In dance terms, a trust is a long-term rehearsal plan. More structure. More intention. More preparation.

The key is not complexity. It is fit.

Beneficiaries and Account Titling

Many assets do not follow your will.

Retirement accounts, life insurance policies, and some bank accounts pass directly to named beneficiaries. If those designations are outdated, incorrect, or missing, your plan breaks down.

Common mistakes include:

- Forgetting to update beneficiaries after life changes
- Naming minors without proper structure
- Leaving defaults in place
- Assuming a will overrides account paperwork

Account titling matters just as much. Joint ownership, individual ownership, and payable-on-death designations all change outcomes.

In dance terms, this is alignment between rehearsal and performance. If your paperwork does not match your intent, the execution fails.

A regular review of beneficiaries is one of the simplest, highest-impact estate planning steps you can take.

Powers of Attorney: Financial Control When You Cannot Act

A power of attorney allows someone you trust to manage financial matters if you cannot.

That includes:

- Paying bills
- Managing accounts
- Handling contracts
- Making financial decisions during incapacity

Without this document, even close family members may be unable to help. Courts may need to step in. Time is lost when clarity matters most.

For dancers, this is especially important during:

- Injury recovery
- Surgery
- Extended travel
- Medical emergencies

In performance terms, a power of attorney is a trusted understudy. You hope they never step in, but you prepare them anyway.

Healthcare Directives: Medical Wishes and Advocacy

Healthcare directives outline your medical preferences and name someone to make healthcare decisions if you cannot.

This includes:

- Treatment preferences
- End-of-life wishes
- Organ donation
- Medical decision-maker

Without a healthcare directive, decisions may fall to people who do not know your values or wishes.

Dancers understand bodily autonomy deeply. You know your body is your instrument. Healthcare directives protect that instrument even when you cannot speak.

In dance terms, this is protecting your body offstage with the same seriousness you bring to performance.

Estate Planning Is Not One-and-Done

Estate planning is a living system.

It should be reviewed when:

- Income changes
- Relationships change
- You move states
- You buy property
- You start or end contracts
- Your goals shift

Perfection is not required. Progress is.

A basic plan done early is far more powerful than a perfect plan delayed forever.

Coach's Perspective

If a coach were talking about estate planning, the message would be blunt.

Prepare before you need it.

Do not leave chaos behind you.

Protect your people.

Handle your business.

Do not assume someone else will fix it.

This is not dramatic work. It is responsible work.

Game Situations and Decision Points

You get injured and cannot manage finances for weeks.

Who steps in?

Your accounts list outdated beneficiaries.

Does your plan still reflect your life?

You assume your family will "figure it out."

Do they have legal authority to do so?

Ignoring these questions does not make them disappear.

Common Performer Mistakes and Financial Parallels

Performers think estate planning is only for the wealthy.

Financially, that leads to unnecessary complications.

Performers delay uncomfortable decisions.

Financially, that shifts burden to loved ones.

Performers assume good intentions are enough.

Financially, paperwork is what actually matters.

Winning the Long Game

Estate planning is an act of care.

It protects your work.

It protects your people.

It protects your values.

The dancers who plan ahead create calm in moments that could otherwise be chaotic. That is leadership beyond the stage.

You do not need to have everything figured out. You need to take the next responsible step.

Athlete Takeaways

- Estate planning is about control, not wealth
- A will creates clarity when emotions run high
- Beneficiaries and account titles matter more than people think
- Powers of attorney and healthcare directives protect you while alive
- Planning early is a gift to yourself and the people you care about

Chapter 24: Talking About Money With Family

Few things are harder than talking about money with the people you care about most.

Not because money is complicated, but because money is emotional. It is tied to identity, sacrifice, fear, pride, and expectations that often go unspoken. For dancers, this can be even more layered. Families may have invested years of time, travel, tuition, costumes, and support into your training. Gratitude, guilt, pressure, and obligation can all show up in the same conversation.

Avoiding money conversations does not protect relationships. It quietly strains them.

Learning how to talk about money with family is part of building a sustainable life beyond performance.

Why These Conversations Feel So Hard

Dance culture teaches discipline, respect, and deference. Many dancers grow up listening more than speaking, trusting authority, and pushing through discomfort. That can make financial conversations with family feel unnatural.

Common internal conflicts show up:

- "They sacrificed so much for me."

- "I don't want to disappoint them."
- "I should be grateful, not ask questions."
- "Talking about money feels selfish."
- "I don't want to create tension."

Silence feels safer in the moment. Over time, it creates confusion, resentment, and misaligned expectations.

Just like in rehearsal, clarity prevents breakdowns later.

Teaching Kids About Money Without Pressure

If you have children or plan to, money conversations start earlier than most people think.

Kids do not need complex financial lessons. They need **exposure**, **language**, and **example**.

Teaching kids about money means:

- Explaining that money is earned, not magical
- Showing that choices have trade-offs
- Normalizing saving, spending, and giving
- Talking openly about mistakes and learning

Simple habits matter:

- Let kids see you budget
- Explain why you say yes or no to purchases
- Involve them in age-appropriate decisions
- Talk about goals, not just rules

In dance terms, this is basic training. You do not wait until advanced choreography to teach posture and alignment. Money skills work the same way.

The goal is not perfection. The goal is confidence and comfort around money.

Supporting Parents and Caregivers

As dancers age, roles often shift.

Parents who once supported you may need help themselves. Caregiving can enter the picture unexpectedly due to health issues, aging, or financial strain. These moments bring emotional weight and financial complexity.

Supporting parents does not automatically mean funding everything. It means:

- Understanding their financial reality
- Knowing what support is expected versus assumed
- Clarifying what you can and cannot provide
- Planning together instead of reacting later

Dancers often feel a strong sense of responsibility. That responsibility needs boundaries to remain healthy.

In performance terms, this is pacing. You cannot give everything in the first section and expect to finish strong.

Managing Expectations and Boundaries

This is where most conflict lives.

Family expectations are often implied, not stated. Money can turn those assumptions into pressure:

- Expectations of financial support
- Assumptions about lifestyle
- Beliefs about "success"
- Opinions about spending, saving, or career choices

Boundaries are not rejection. They are clarity.

Healthy boundaries sound like:

- "I want to help, but here's what I can realistically do."
- "I'm working toward long-term stability, not short-term appearances."
- "I need to make decisions that protect my future."
- "I'm open to discussing this, but I need time to think."

Boundaries protect relationships from resentment. Without them, dancers often overextend financially to avoid discomfort, then pay for it later.

In dance terms, boundaries are spacing. Without spacing, collisions happen.

Navigating Financial Conversations Without Conflict

You do not need to win these conversations. You need to navigate them well.

Some principles help:

- Choose timing intentionally. Not during stress or crisis if possible.
- Speak from your perspective, not accusation.
- Be honest about uncertainty. You do not need all the answers.
- Listen fully. People want to be heard more than corrected.
- Separate emotion from logistics when possible.

Money conversations rarely go perfectly. That is normal. What matters is returning to them instead of avoiding them permanently.

Just like rehearsal, communication improves with reps.

When Family and Money Get Entangled

Dance careers often blur personal and financial lines.

Family may:

- Pay for training

- Help with housing
- Support transitions between contracts
- Provide emergency assistance

Gratitude is appropriate. Dependency without clarity is dangerous.

If family support exists, it helps to discuss:

- Is this a gift or a loan?
- Are there expectations attached?
- Is this temporary or ongoing?
- How does this affect long-term planning?

Unspoken assumptions create stress on both sides. Clear conversations reduce misunderstandings and preserve respect.

Coach's Perspective

If a coach were addressing this, the tone would be direct.

Handle hard conversations early.

Protect relationships with clarity.

Do not avoid discomfort and call it kindness.

Communicate like a professional.

Respect yourself and the people around you.

Avoiding the conversation does not make it easier later.

Game Situations and Decision Points

Your family assumes you will help financially.

Do you clarify expectations now or let pressure build?

A parent needs support.

Do you help reactively or plan intentionally?

You feel judged for your financial choices.

Do you shut down or explain your long-term vision?

These moments shape both finances and relationships.

Common Performer Mistakes and Financial Parallels

Performers avoid difficult conversations.

Financially, that leads to hidden stress.

Performers overextend to please others.

Financially, that delays stability.

Performers confuse gratitude with obligation.

Financially, that creates long-term strain.

Winning the Long Game

Money conversations with family are part of adulthood, not a failure of independence.

Handled well, they build trust.

Handled poorly, they quietly damage relationships.

You do not need to be perfect. You need to be honest, respectful, and consistent.

Just like dance, longevity comes from balance, communication, and intentional choices.

Athlete Takeaways

- Money conversations protect relationships, not threaten them
- Teach kids early through example, not pressure
- Supporting family requires boundaries, not sacrifice of your future
- Clear expectations prevent long-term resentment
- Difficult conversations get easier with reps

Part VI: Sustaining Success

Sustaining success in dance is never about one performance, one contract, or one good year. It is about what you build quietly over time, when the spotlight is inconsistent and the future is uncertain. Money works the same way.

This final section of the book is not about flashy wins or dramatic breakthroughs. It is about staying grounded, solvent, and confident through long careers, transitions, and seasons when momentum feels slow. Most dancers do not struggle because they lack talent or work ethic. They struggle because no one teaches them how to **maintain stability while life keeps changing**.

Sustaining success means learning how to manage money when:

- Income fluctuates
- Opportunities come and go
- Injuries interrupt plans
- Career paths evolve
- Identity shifts beyond performance

The goal is not to avoid change. The goal is to be prepared for it.

Why Sustainability Matters More Than Peak Moments

Dance culture celebrates peaks. Big roles. Big shows. Big moments. But peaks are temporary by nature.

Financial stability is built in the valleys.

The months between contracts.

The years when priorities shift.

The seasons when income slows down.

The transitions out of full-time performance.

Dancers who survive and thrive long term understand this truth early: **you cannot live financially as if every year will be your best year**.

Sustaining success means building systems that work whether things are exciting or quiet.

Systems Over Motivation

Motivation fades. Systems remain.

In dance, you do not rely on inspiration to show up to class. You rely on routine. Warm-ups. Technique. Conditioning. Recovery. The same principle applies to money.

Sustainable financial systems include:

- Automatic saving and investing
- Clear spending boundaries
- Regular check-ins, not constant monitoring
- Long-term planning that adapts as life changes

When systems are in place, you do not need to make perfect decisions every time. The structure does the heavy lifting.

This is how professionals last.

Redefining Success Over Time

Early in a career, success might mean booking work or earning enough to stay afloat. Later, success often looks different:

- Stability instead of scramble
- Flexibility instead of urgency
- Choice instead of survival
- Peace instead of pressure

Money plays a quiet but powerful role in that shift.

When finances are unstable, every decision feels urgent. When finances are solid, you can make thoughtful choices aligned with your values instead of fear.

Sustaining success means allowing your definition of winning to evolve.

Managing Transitions Without Panic

Most dancers experience multiple transitions:

- From student to professional
- From full-time performer to hybrid career
- From performing to teaching, directing, or creating
- From one city or company to another
- From dance-centered identity to a broader life

Transitions are not failures. They are expected.

Financial stress during transitions usually comes from lack of preparation, not lack of ability. Emergency funds, diversified income, and realistic planning turn transitions into manageable phases instead of crises.

Sustainability is what allows you to move forward without burning bridges or yourself.

Staying Disciplined When No One Is Watching

Early in dance training, structure is external. Class schedules. Directors. Rehearsals. Deadlines.

Later, discipline becomes internal.

The same is true financially. No one grades your budget. No one checks if you saved this month. No one tells you when to plan for retirement or insurance or taxes.

Sustaining success requires self-leadership.

That means:

- Reviewing finances even when nothing feels urgent
- Making conservative choices during good years
- Avoiding lifestyle inflation driven by comparison
- Protecting future flexibility, not just current comfort

This is professional maturity.

The Long View

Dance teaches patience, repetition, and respect for the process. Those lessons apply directly to money.

There is no single decision that guarantees success. There are hundreds of small, mostly unremarkable choices that compound over time.

Sustaining success is not exciting. It is effective.

It is showing up prepared.

It is managing risk.

It is planning beyond the next opportunity.

It is building a life that supports your art, not one that collapses when the stage changes.

Final Perspective

Your career will evolve. Your income will change. Your priorities will shift.

Money should support that evolution, not fight it.

Sustaining success means you are not just surviving dance. You are building a life that works during and after it.

That is the real win.

Chapter 25: Advisors, Scams, and Long-Term Success

Long dance careers are rarely built alone. Even the most disciplined performers rely on teachers, coaches, physical therapists, and mentors to stay healthy and improve over time. Financial success works the same way. Knowing **when to ask for help**, **who to trust**, and **how to protect yourself** is just as important as talent or work ethic.

This chapter brings everything together. It is about learning how to use advisors wisely, avoid costly traps, and build habits that support success long after the applause fades.

When to Seek Professional Help

Many dancers wait too long to ask for financial help. Others seek it too early from the wrong people. The goal is not to outsource responsibility. The goal is to add support when the decisions become bigger than simple budgeting.

You may want professional help when:

- Your income becomes inconsistent or increases quickly
- You are juggling multiple contracts, freelance work, or side income
- Taxes feel confusing or stressful
- You are unsure how to invest beyond basic savings
- You want a long-term plan instead of reacting year to year

- You are approaching a major transition, such as leaving full-time performance

Seeking help is not a sign of weakness. It is a sign of maturity. Just as you would not self-diagnose a serious injury, you should not guess your way through complex financial decisions.

Types of Financial Advisors

Not all advisors do the same job, and not all are right for dancers. Understanding the differences helps you choose wisely.

Financial Planners

These advisors focus on the big picture. Budgeting, saving, investing, taxes, insurance, and long-term goals. A good planner helps you build a system, not just pick investments.

Investment Advisors

These professionals focus primarily on managing investments. They may not help much with cash flow, career planning, or taxes unless it is part of their service model.

Insurance Professionals

They specialize in risk protection such as health, disability, life, and liability insurance. These areas are critical for dancers, but insurance should fit into a broader plan, not exist in isolation.

Tax Professionals

Accountants and tax preparers help with compliance, filing, and tax strategy. This becomes especially important for dancers with freelance income, touring work, or multiple states involved.

The best outcomes usually come when professionals collaborate or when one advisor understands how to coordinate the whole picture.

Recognizing Scams and Bad Advice

Dancers are often targeted because of income swings, career uncertainty, and lack of formal financial education. Scams rarely look like scams at first. They look like shortcuts.

Red flags include:

- Guaranteed returns or promises of safety
- Pressure to act quickly
- Fear-based language about missing out
- Advice that discourages second opinions
- Products that are overly complex and poorly explained
- Someone who focuses more on selling than teaching

Bad advice often sounds confident but ignores your reality. If an approach does not account for variable income, career risk, or long-term sustainability, it is not designed for performers.

If you do not understand how something works, you should not be investing in it.

Ten Common Financial Mistakes Dancers Make

1. Treating good years as permanent
2. Failing to save during busy seasons
3. Ignoring taxes until they become a crisis
4. Carrying high-interest debt for lifestyle reasons
5. Confusing income with financial security
6. Chasing fast wins instead of steady progress
7. Avoiding insurance to save short-term cash
8. Trusting advice without understanding incentives
9. Comparing finances to other performers
10. Waiting too long to plan for life beyond dance

These mistakes are not caused by laziness. They are caused by lack of guidance and pressure to survive in the moment.

Ten Rules for Long-Term Success

1. Build systems, not reactions
2. Save consistently, not occasionally
3. Protect your income before chasing growth
4. Spend intentionally, not emotionally
5. Keep decisions simple and repeatable
6. Ask questions until you understand
7. Plan for change, not certainty
8. Separate identity from income
9. Measure progress over years, not months
10. Stay disciplined when no one is watching

These rules are not exciting, but they work. They are the financial equivalent of technique, conditioning, and recovery. They do not guarantee stardom, but they dramatically increase the odds of stability and freedom.

Using Advisors the Right Way

The best advisor relationships are collaborative. You bring honesty and effort. They bring structure, education, and perspective.

A good advisor:

- Explains decisions clearly
- Encourages questions
- Helps you think long term
- Respects your career reality
- Prioritizes sustainability over flash

No advisor can replace discipline. No advisor can make decisions for you.

But the right one can help you avoid mistakes that cost years of progress.

Winning the Long Game

Dance teaches patience, repetition, and respect for fundamentals. Financial success demands the same qualities.

There will be seasons of momentum and seasons of uncertainty. There will be contracts that excite you and transitions that challenge you. Money does not remove those realities, but it determines how much control you have when they arrive.

Long-term success is not about avoiding mistakes entirely. It is about limiting the damage when mistakes happen and staying consistent long enough for progress to compound.

Athlete Takeaways

- Play the long game, not the highlight reel
- Ask for help before problems become injuries
- Protect your income like you protect your body
- Do not confuse confidence with competence
- Stay disciplined when the spotlight moves on

This chapter closes the book with one final reminder. Dance careers are unpredictable. Your financial foundation does not have to be.

Chapter 26: Losing the Schedule and Rebuilding Structure

One of the most jarring transitions dancers face is not physical. It is structural.

For years, your life was organized for you. Class times were fixed. Rehearsals were mandatory. Call sheets told you where to be and when. Someone else decided the rhythm of your day, your week, your season. That structure was not optional. It was enforced.

Then, almost overnight, it disappears.

No more daily class posted on the board. No more rehearsal blocks. No one checking attendance. No director setting the tempo of your week. What replaces it is freedom, but freedom without structure often becomes chaos. And that chaos quietly spills into money.

This chapter is about understanding why life feels harder when no one is setting your calendar and how rebuilding structure is essential not only for your career and identity, but for your financial stability.

Why Life Gets Harder When No One Is Setting Your Calendar

In dance, discipline is external first. You show up because you have to. Over time, that external discipline becomes internal. Or at least, it feels like it does.

But when the external pressure disappears, many dancers discover something uncomfortable. The discipline was real, but it was supported by structure they no longer have.

Without a schedule:

- Days blur together
- Decisions multiply
- Small choices become exhausting
- Motivation becomes inconsistent

This is not a personal failure. It is a systems problem.

Structure reduces decision fatigue. When rehearsal is from 10 to 2, you do not debate whether to train. You simply go. When paychecks arrive on predictable dates, budgeting is easier. When income is irregular and your calendar is wide open, everything requires conscious effort.

Money struggles often begin here, not because of bad intentions, but because structure quietly vanished.

From Mandatory Workouts to Optional Discipline

In training environments, discipline is non-negotiable. You train whether you feel like it or not. You stretch whether you are motivated or not. You condition because it is part of the system.

After dance, discipline becomes optional. That is a dangerous shift.

Optional discipline sounds like:

- "I will save when I make more money"
- "I will track expenses next month"
- "I will think about investing later"
- "I will deal with taxes when they are due"

Nothing is forcing action anymore. And without systems, good intentions fade.

This is why many dancers feel productive but still fall behind financially. They are working, auditioning, teaching, freelancing, but without a structure that supports consistent financial behavior.

Discipline without structure is exhausting. Structure without discipline does not last. You need both.

How Lack of Structure Quietly Breaks Financial Habits

The breakdown is rarely dramatic. It happens quietly.

You stop checking your account regularly.

You miss a savings transfer.

You delay opening important mail.

You forget estimated taxes.

You spend more freely during busy months and scramble during slow ones.

None of these feel like major mistakes. But over time, they compound.

Financial habits depend on rhythm. When the rhythm disappears, habits weaken.

In dance, missing one class does not end a career. Missing class consistently does. Money works the same way. One missed savings month is not fatal. A year without structure creates lasting consequences.

The most dangerous part is that this breakdown often feels emotional. Dancers blame motivation, burnout, or confidence, when the real issue is lack of a system.

Replacing Practice Schedules With Personal Systems

You do not need the same structure you had before. You need a new one that fits your current reality.

The goal is not rigidity. The goal is consistency.

Personal systems might include:

- Weekly financial check-ins on the same day
- Automatic transfers for savings and taxes
- A fixed day each month for bill review

- A set time block for career administration
- A quarterly review of income, expenses, and goals

These systems replace the old rehearsal schedule. They become the new baseline.

Think of them as technique for adulthood. They are not exciting, but they support everything else.

Creating a Financial Training Plan

Just as you once followed a training plan, your money needs one too.

A financial training plan answers:

- When do I review my money?
- What happens automatically?
- What requires my attention?
- How do I prepare for slow periods?
- How do I measure progress?

This plan does not need to be complicated. Simple systems executed consistently outperform complex plans abandoned under stress.

For example:

- Income arrives, a percentage automatically goes to savings
- A separate account holds tax money
- Bills are automated where possible
- One weekly check-in keeps awareness high

That is structure. Not perfection. Not intensity. Just consistency.

Structure Supports Identity, Not Just Money

Losing structure affects more than finances. It impacts identity.

Dance gave you:

- A place to be
- A role to play
- A daily purpose

When that disappears, money often becomes a proxy for worth. Income feels personal. Slow months feel like failure. Comparison increases.

Structure stabilizes identity. When you know what your week looks like, what your priorities are, and how your money is handled, self-worth becomes less volatile.

You are no longer reacting to each gig or lull. You are operating within a system.

Discipline Is Harder Without an Audience

In the studio, effort is visible. Someone is watching. Corrections are immediate. Progress is external.

With money, no one is clapping. No one is correcting your form. The work is invisible.

That is why discipline breaks down so easily.

The solution is not more willpower. It is accountability and structure. Tools, reminders, advisors, checklists, and systems become the new mirrors.

They show you the truth before small problems grow.

Building a Schedule That Works for Real Life

Your new schedule will not look like your old one. That is okay.

What matters is that:

- Money tasks have a place
- Decisions are not left to chance
- You remove as much friction as possible
- You build routines that survive busy seasons

Structure is not about control. It is about freedom. When systems handle the basics, your energy is freed for creativity, performance, and growth.

Winning Without a Choreographer

Eventually, every dancer must self-direct. The same is true financially.

No one is coming to enforce your schedule. No one is handing you a plan. That does not mean you are alone. It means responsibility has shifted.

Those who rebuild structure early regain stability faster. Those who delay often spend years feeling behind without knowing why.

You do not need to do everything at once. You need to start.

Athlete Takeaways

- Structure creates discipline when motivation fades
- Systems beat willpower every time
- Money habits need rhythm, not intensity
- Schedule your finances like you once scheduled class
- Freedom works best when it is supported by structure

Rebuilding structure is not going backward. It is how you move forward with control, confidence, and longevity.

Chapter 27: From Teammates to Coworkers

One of the hardest transitions after sports or performance is not learning a new skill. It is learning a new environment.

For most of your athletic life, you operated inside a team structure. Roles were clear. Authority was visible. Expectations were spoken out loud. Feedback was constant. If something went wrong, you watched film, got corrected, and tried again the next day.

Then you step into the workplace.

Suddenly, the rules are different. The language is different. The power structure is less obvious. Feedback is inconsistent or missing altogether. Success is harder to measure. And the people around you are no longer teammates moving toward the same scoreboard.

This chapter is about why the workplace often feels foreign to former athletes and performers, and how misunderstanding this shift can quietly stall income growth, confidence, and long-term career stability.

Why the Workplace Feels Foreign After Sports

Athletes are trained in clarity.

You know who the coach is.

You know who decides playing time.

You know what good performance looks like.

You know when you messed up.

Workplaces rarely operate that way.

In most jobs, expectations are implied, not stated. Authority is layered, not singular. Performance is evaluated privately, sometimes subjectively. Outcomes depend on factors outside your control.

For someone raised in a performance-based environment, this can feel disorienting. You may work harder than everyone else and still feel invisible. You may follow instructions perfectly and still miss an unspoken expectation.

This disconnect is not because you lack ability. It is because the environment rewards different behaviors than sports did.

Authority Without Coaches

In sports, authority is obvious. The coach sets the system. You may disagree, but you know who is in charge.

In the workplace, authority is fragmented.

Your direct manager may not control your compensation.

Human resources may influence decisions without knowing your work.

Executives may set priorities that conflict with your department's goals.

This creates confusion for former athletes who are used to a clear chain of command.

Many athletes assume effort alone earns trust and opportunity. In sports, that is often true. In the workplace, visibility, communication, and alignment matter just as much as effort.

If you are waiting for someone to notice how hard you work, you may wait a long time.

Feedback Without Film

In athletics, feedback is constant. Film does not lie. Corrections are specific. You know exactly what to fix.

In the workplace, feedback is sporadic or vague.

You might hear:

- "You're doing fine"
- "Keep it up"
- "Let's circle back later"

Or worse, nothing at all.

Without feedback, athletes often default to self-criticism. They assume silence means failure. Or they push harder without knowing if effort is being directed correctly.

This creates two risks.

First, burnout. You are sprinting without knowing where the finish line is.

Second, stagnation. You repeat behaviors that are not rewarded because no one tells you otherwise.

Learning to ask for feedback is a new skill. Learning to interpret indirect feedback is even harder. But both are essential for career and income growth.

Politics, Ambiguity, and Unclear Expectations

Sports culture values directness. Work culture often avoids it.

Decisions may be influenced by:

- Relationships
- Perception
- Timing
- Office dynamics
- Budget cycles

None of these show up on a stat sheet.

For athletes, this can feel unfair or dishonest. The instinct is to disengage or dismiss politics entirely. That instinct can be costly.

Ignoring workplace dynamics does not make you principled. It makes you less informed.

Understanding how decisions are made does not require compromising your values. It requires awareness.

Career advancement often depends on:

- Being trusted, not just talented
- Being reliable, not just intense
- Being clear, not just compliant
- Being aligned with priorities, not just busy

These are skills athletes were rarely taught, but they can be learned.

How This Impacts Income Growth

Income growth in sports is tied to performance. Income growth at work is tied to perception, timing, and negotiation.

This is where many former athletes struggle.

They assume raises come from effort.

They assume promotions come from loyalty.

They assume good work speaks for itself.

In reality:

- Raises often require asking
- Promotions require advocacy
- Opportunities go to those who communicate value clearly

If you are uncomfortable discussing money, your income will lag behind your contribution.

Athletes are taught to let coaches handle placement and reward. In adult careers, you are expected to manage your own trajectory.

That includes:

- Understanding how compensation works
- Tracking your results
- Articulating your impact

- Advocating for yourself without apology

This is not ego. It is professional responsibility.

Career Stability Requires New Fundamentals

Athletic careers are structured around seasons. Work careers are continuous.

Without clear checkpoints, it is easy to drift.

Career stability comes from:

- Skill development
- Relationship building
- Financial planning
- Long-term positioning

Former athletes often focus on effort and ignore strategy. They outwork problems instead of redesigning the system.

That approach works in training. It breaks down in careers.

Stability requires patience, communication, and adaptability. It requires understanding that success is not always visible in the short term.

Rebuilding the Team Mentality

One of the most painful shifts is losing the sense of team.

Coworkers are not teammates in the same way. Incentives differ. Goals may conflict. Loyalty is less certain.

This can feel isolating.

The solution is not expecting work to feel like sports. It is building connection intentionally.

Mentors replace coaches.

Peers replace teammates.

Professional networks replace locker rooms.

These relationships do not form automatically. They require effort outside of your job description.

But they matter deeply. Most career opportunities come through people, not postings.

Translating Athletic Strengths to Work Success

Athletes bring powerful strengths into the workplace:

- Discipline
- Coachability
- Resilience
- Accountability
- Work ethic

The challenge is translating them correctly.

Discipline becomes consistency, not just intensity.

Coachability becomes adaptability, not just obedience.

Resilience becomes emotional regulation, not just toughness.

When these strengths are applied intentionally, athletes thrive.

When they are applied blindly, athletes feel frustrated and undervalued.

Financial Consequences of the Transition

When career progress stalls, financial stress follows.

Income growth slows.

Benefits are misunderstood.

Retirement savings are delayed.

Confidence erodes.

This is why career education and financial education must be linked.

Understanding the workplace helps you:

- Increase earning power
- Reduce volatility

- Plan for long-term goals
- Make informed financial decisions

Money problems are often career problems in disguise.

Learning a New Game Without a Rulebook

No one hands you a workplace playbook. Most people learn by trial and error.

Former athletes often expect clarity that never arrives. They wait for direction instead of designing their own path.

The ones who succeed learn to:

- Ask better questions
- Seek mentors
- Observe power dynamics
- Communicate value
- Plan financially alongside career moves

This is not abandoning your athletic identity. It is evolving it.

Athlete Takeaways

- Work is a different game with different rules
- Effort matters, but visibility and communication matter too
- Feedback must often be requested, not expected
- Income growth requires advocacy, not patience alone
- Career stability comes from strategy, not just hard work

Moving from teammates to coworkers is not a downgrade. It is a transition. Those who learn the new system early build stronger careers, steadier finances, and a more sustainable life beyond competition.

Chapter 28: When No One Is Watching Anymore

For most of your athletic life, someone was always watching.

A coach tracked attendance.

A strength coach monitored effort.

A teammate noticed when you skipped reps.

A scoreboard told the truth at the end of the day.

Even on bad days, accountability existed. You could not hide. You either showed up or you did not.

Then the sport ends.

No one checks your calendar.

No one reviews your film.

No one tells you when effort slips.

And that is where many former athletes struggle most. Not because they lack discipline, but because discipline was always reinforced externally. When that structure disappears, a gap opens. What you do inside that gap determines everything that follows, including your money decisions.

The Discipline Gap After Accountability Disappears

Athletes are trained to respond to structure, not create it.

Practice times are set.

Training plans are built for you.

Seasons dictate intensity and recovery.

When that system disappears, the assumption is that discipline automatically transfers. In reality, discipline changes form.

In sports, discipline is enforced.

In adult life, discipline is chosen.

That difference matters.

Without external accountability, small lapses become habits. Skipped workouts become skipped planning. Missed deadlines become delayed decisions. Financial tasks get postponed because nothing feels urgent.

The discipline gap does not show up dramatically. It shows up quietly. And by the time it becomes visible, damage has already occurred.

Why Former Athletes Self-Sabotage Without Pressure

Self-sabotage is rarely intentional.

Former athletes are used to pressure creating clarity. Big games sharpen focus. Consequences force execution. When pressure disappears, motivation often drops with it.

This leads to subtle self-sabotage patterns:

- Avoiding decisions instead of making imperfect ones
- Spending for comfort instead of planning for growth
- Delaying savings because retirement feels abstract
- Ignoring small financial issues until they become big ones

Without pressure, there is no urgency. Without urgency, effort fades.

Athletes are not lazy. They are misaligned. Their nervous system was trained to perform under observation. When no one is watching, the system shuts down instead of recalibrating.

This is why former athletes often feel stuck even when they are capable.

Comfort Versus Growth Decisions

In sports, comfort is dangerous.

Comfort means your opponent is catching up.

Comfort means intensity is slipping.

Comfort means growth has stalled.

In adult life, comfort feels earned. And it often is.

After years of grinding, many former athletes finally experience freedom. No early workouts. No constant evaluation. No pressure to prove anything.

That freedom can become a trap.

Comfort decisions often look like:

- Upgrading lifestyle before income stabilizes
- Choosing convenience over long-term planning
- Avoiding financial discomfort like budgeting or tracking spending
- Staying in roles that feel safe but limit growth

Growth decisions often feel uncomfortable:

- Saying no to lifestyle inflation
- Saving when others are spending
- Investing without immediate gratification
- Asking for raises or changing careers

Without a coach pushing you, comfort wins by default.

This is not a character flaw. It is a structural issue. Growth now requires self-imposed pressure.

Translating "Grind Culture" Into Adult Life

Athletes know how to grind. The problem is that grind culture does not translate cleanly into adulthood.

Grinding in sports has a clear goal.

Grinding in life often does not.

If you apply grind without direction, you get burnout, not progress.

Many former athletes stay busy but stagnant. They work hard but without a plan. They hustle but without leverage. They exhaust themselves without moving forward financially.

Adult discipline is not about doing more. It is about doing the right things consistently.

That means:

- Building systems instead of relying on willpower
- Automating savings instead of forcing discipline
- Scheduling planning time instead of waiting for motivation
- Creating rules for money when emotions are high

Grind culture must evolve into systems culture.

Systems do not care how you feel. They keep working when motivation fades.

Why Money Mistakes Show Up Years Later

Financial mistakes rarely hurt immediately.

Skipping savings this year does not feel painful.

Carrying a balance feels manageable at first.

Lifestyle upgrades feel deserved.

The cost shows up later.

Years later, you realize:

- Your savings is behind where it should be
- Debt limits your flexibility
- Career transitions feel riskier
- Stress increases as options shrink

Athletes are used to immediate feedback. Miss a shot, you know it. Financial feedback is delayed.

This delay is why former athletes are often shocked by their financial situation in their thirties or forties. The mistakes were not sudden. They were cumulative.

No one was watching. No one blew the whistle. The consequences arrived quietly.

The Absence of a Scoreboard

Sports provide constant measurement.

Time.

Score.

Rankings.

Stats.

Adult life removes the scoreboard.

Without measurement, it is hard to know if you are winning or losing. This leads to comparison traps. You judge success by titles, houses, cars, or social media signals.

Those are poor scoreboards.

Financial health requires a different measurement system:

- Cash flow stability
- Emergency savings
- Debt control
- Investment progress
- Career optionality

If you do not track these, you are guessing.

And guessing leads to drift.

Rebuilding Accountability Without a Team

The solution is not recreating your sport. It is recreating accountability.

That can look like:

- Scheduled money check-ins
- Automatic contributions
- External advisors or mentors
- Clear financial goals with deadlines
- Written rules for spending and saving

Accountability does not require pressure. It requires visibility.

When your actions are visible to yourself or others, behavior changes.

Former athletes thrive when accountability returns, even if it is self-imposed.

Discipline as Identity, Not Environment

The most successful former athletes make one key shift.

They stop seeing discipline as something imposed by a system and start seeing it as part of who they are.

Discipline becomes identity-driven.

You save because that is how you operate.

You plan because that is how you compete.

You delay gratification because you understand long games.

This shift takes time. It also takes intention.

You cannot wait for motivation. You must build habits that function without it.

The Quiet Power of Boring Consistency

No one applauds consistency.

No one celebrates automatic savings.

No one praises skipping upgrades.

No one notices steady investing.

But consistency compounds.

Former athletes often want intensity. Financial success rewards repetition.

The ones who win long-term are not the most aggressive. They are the most consistent.

When No One Is Watching, Character Shows Up

Sports teach you how to perform under pressure. Life tests how you behave without it.

When no one is watching:

- Do you still train your finances
- Do you still make disciplined choices
- Do you still plan for the future
- Do you still protect your options

These moments define outcomes far more than highlight plays.

Athlete Takeaways

- Discipline changes when accountability disappears
- Comfort decisions feel good now but cost later
- Grind must evolve into systems
- Financial mistakes are quiet before they are painful
- Consistency wins when no one is watching

When the crowd leaves and the lights go off, the work does not stop. It simply changes. The athletes who understand that build lives that last long after the uniform comes off.

Chapter 29: Redefining Winning After the Uniform Comes Off

For most of your life as an athlete, winning was clearly defined.

You knew the rules.

You knew the scoreboard.

You knew exactly what success looked like.

Wins and losses were public. Rankings were visible. Roles were earned. Progress was measurable. Even when things were hard, the target was clear.

Then the uniform comes off.

And suddenly, winning becomes vague.

There is no scoreboard.

No rankings.

No clear season.

That lack of definition creates one of the most dangerous transitions former athletes face. When performance is no longer clearly measured, many people replace it with something easier to see.

Status.

Why Chasing Status Replaces Chasing Performance

Athletes are wired to compete. That does not disappear when sport ends. What changes is what you are competing for.

Without a clear performance metric, status fills the gap.

Titles.

Income.

Homes.

Cars.

Visible success.

These things are easy to compare. They create a sense of progress. They provide external validation similar to what sports once gave you.

The problem is that status is a poor substitute for performance.

Performance is about execution, growth, and sustainability.

Status is about perception.

When former athletes chase status, decisions shift:

- Spending increases faster than stability
- Career moves prioritize optics over alignment
- Financial pressure grows quietly behind the scenes
- Comparison replaces self-assessment

Status feels like winning, but it rarely leads to long-term fulfillment.

Income Versus Fulfillment

Income is important. It provides security, options, and freedom. But income alone is not the same as success.

Many former athletes fall into the trap of treating income like a final score.

If the number is higher this year than last year, they assume they are winning.

But income without fulfillment creates a hollow victory.

You can earn more and feel less satisfied.

You can advance and feel more trapped.

You can succeed on paper and feel lost internally.

Athletes understand this better than most. You have been on teams that won games but felt broken. You have also experienced seasons where growth mattered more than the record.

Fulfillment comes from alignment. It comes from knowing your effort supports the life you want, not just the image you project.

Titles, Houses, Cars, and Comparison Traps

In the absence of a scoreboard, comparison becomes constant.

Former athletes often compare:

- Job titles
- Salary levels
- Home size
- Cars and lifestyle upgrades

These markers are visible, so they feel meaningful. But they are also misleading.

Titles do not tell you about stress levels.

Houses do not reveal debt.

Cars do not reflect savings.

Income does not show burnout.

Comparison traps push people to make financial decisions based on appearance rather than strategy.

Buying too much house too early.

Upgrading lifestyle before cash flow stabilizes.

Taking roles that look impressive but drain energy.

In sports, chasing highlights instead of fundamentals gets exposed quickly. In life, chasing status can take years to reveal its cost.

By the time it does options are limited.

The Hidden Cost of Status-Based Decisions

Status-based decisions create pressure that does not show up immediately.

Higher fixed expenses reduce flexibility.

Debt limits career choices.

Lifestyle expectations become hard to reverse.

Former athletes often underestimate this because they are confident in their ability to work harder later. That confidence was rewarded in sports. Financially, it can be dangerous.

You cannot outwork structural pressure forever.

The goal is not to avoid success. It is to define it correctly.

What Success Actually Looks Like in Your 30s and 40s

Success evolves.

In your early years, success might look like momentum.

In your thirties, it often looks like stability.

In your forties, it looks like options.

True success for former athletes often includes:

- Predictable cash flow
- Low financial stress
- Career flexibility
- Time autonomy
- Physical and mental health
- Strong relationships

These outcomes are rarely flashy. They are rarely posted online. But they are powerful.

Athletes who redefine winning early build lives that support them instead of trapping them.

Building a New Scoreboard

If you do not define winning, society will do it for you.

A new scoreboard must be intentional.

Instead of asking:

- How do I look?

- How do I compare?
- What will people think?

Start asking:

- How stable is my cash flow?
- How much flexibility do I have?
- How stressed am I about money?
- How aligned is my work with my values?
- How prepared am I for change?

These are performance metrics, not status markers.

They reward discipline, planning, and consistency, the same traits that made you successful as an athlete.

The Shift From External Validation to Internal Standards

Sports trained you to seek feedback externally.

Coaches.

Teammates.

Fans.

Adult life requires a shift inward.

You must decide what winning means.

You must decide what tradeoffs are worth it.

You must decide when enough is enough.

This is uncomfortable for many former athletes. External validation was clear and constant. Internal standards require honesty.

But once established, they are far more stable.

Letting Go of the Old Identity Without Losing the Edge

Redefining winning does not mean losing competitiveness.

It means redirecting it.

Instead of competing for attention, you compete for progress.

Instead of chasing status, you chase sustainability.

Instead of proving yourself, you build for yourself.

The edge remains. The target changes.

Long-Term Thinking Beats Short-Term Applause

Athletes understand seasons. Financial success works the same way.

One good year does not define a career.

One big purchase does not define success.

One promotion does not guarantee fulfillment.

What matters is trajectory.

Are you moving toward freedom or pressure?

Are you building options or obligations?

Are your decisions expanding or shrinking your future?

Winning is not a moment. It is a pattern.

Choosing Fulfillment Without Apology

Former athletes sometimes feel guilty choosing fulfillment over status.

They feel like they should want more titles, more money, more recognition.

You do not owe anyone a performance after your sport ends.

You owe yourself a life that works.

Fulfillment is not quitting. It is clarity.

Athlete Takeaways

- Status is visible, performance is sustainable
- Income matters, fulfillment determines longevity
- Comparison creates pressure, not progress
- Define your own scoreboard early
- Winning long-term means building options, not appearances

When the uniform comes off, the game does not end. The rules change. The athletes who redefine winning on their own terms build lives that are not just successful, but steady, flexible, and deeply satisfying.

Chapter 30: Staying Connected Without Living in the Past

Every athlete knows the feeling of belonging.

You were part of something bigger than yourself.

A team.

A locker room.

A shared mission.

Even on bad days, you were not alone. There were teammates next to you. Coaches pushing you. A structure that gave your effort meaning.

When the uniform comes off, that connection often disappears overnight.

No locker room.

No daily check-ins.

No built-in accountability.

For many former athletes, this loss is more disorienting than the loss of competition itself.

The Role of Community After Sports

Sports create automatic community.

You do not have to search for it. You are assigned to it. Practice, travel, meetings, and competition force interaction. Relationships form through shared stress, sacrifice, and repetition.

Adult life does not work that way.

Community becomes optional.

Connection becomes intentional.

This shift catches many former athletes off guard. Without realizing it, they move from constant connection to quiet isolation. Work becomes transactional. Friendships become sporadic. Conversations lose depth.

The absence of a team creates a vacuum. If it is not filled intentionally, it often fills with loneliness, frustration, or disengagement.

Why Isolation Hits Former Athletes Hard

Athletes are not used to being alone with their thoughts.

Your days were structured. Your goals were clear. Your feedback was immediate. When something went wrong, you had people around you who understood exactly what you were dealing with.

After sports, isolation creeps in quietly.

You are surrounded by people, but not teammates.

You are busy, but not connected.

You are successful, but not supported.

Isolation is especially dangerous because it often looks like independence.

Former athletes are conditioned to handle things on their own. To push through. To not complain. That mindset works in training. In life, it can create distance.

Isolation is not weakness. It is a signal that something important is missing.

Mentorship as the New Coach Relationship

One of the biggest losses after sports is coaching.

Not instruction, but perspective.

Coaches see the whole picture. They hold you accountable. They challenge blind spots. They remind you who you are when confidence dips.

Mentorship fills that role in adult life.

A mentor does not replace a coach. They provide something different but equally valuable:

- Perspective from experience
- Honest feedback without competition
- Guidance during transitions
- Accountability without authority

Many former athletes wait too long to seek mentorship because they believe they should already have things figured out.

The reality is simple. The best performers in any field seek guidance continuously.

New Locker Rooms Do Not Look Like Old Ones

One of the biggest mistakes former athletes make is searching for the same locker room they left.

It will not exist.

New locker rooms look different:

- Professional communities
- Industry groups
- Faith communities
- Volunteer organizations
- Small peer groups with shared values

The connection is not automatic. You have to show up consistently. You have to contribute. You have to invest before it feels comfortable.

This is hard for athletes because sports trained you to earn belonging through performance. Adult communities often require vulnerability and patience first.

Finding Purpose Without the Team

Sports gave you purpose by default.

Your role mattered. Your effort mattered. Wins and losses mattered. Purpose was external and obvious.

After sports, purpose becomes internal.

This transition can feel unsettling. Without a clear role, many former athletes drift. They stay busy but feel disconnected from meaning.

Purpose does not arrive all at once. It develops through:

- Contribution
- Service
- Growth
- Alignment

Purpose often shows up when you use what sports gave you in new ways. Leadership. Discipline. Resilience. Teaching. Mentoring. Building.

The mistake is waiting for purpose to feel like it did in sports. It will not. It will feel quieter, but deeper.

Healthy Nostalgia Versus Being Stuck

Remembering your playing days is not a problem.

Living in them is.

Healthy nostalgia honors the past without using it as an escape. It recognizes what sports gave you while allowing you to grow beyond it.

Being stuck looks different:

- Constantly reliving old highlights
- Defining yourself only by what you used to do
- Comparing every current experience to your playing days
- Avoiding new challenges because they feel smaller

Sports were a chapter, not the whole book.

Former athletes who struggle most are often the ones who have not allowed themselves to evolve.

You can respect who you were without limiting who you can become.

Letting Identity Expand

During sports, your identity was narrow by necessity.

You were an athlete first. Everything else was secondary.

After sports, identity needs room to expand.

You can be:

- A professional
- A parent
- A mentor
- A leader
- A builder
- A learner

Holding onto a single identity too tightly creates resistance to growth. Expansion does not mean abandonment. It means addition.

The discipline and edge that made you successful in sports do not disappear. They simply get applied differently.

Building Forward-Looking Relationships

Former athletes sometimes gravitate only toward people who knew them as athletes.

That feels safe. It reinforces identity. It validates the past.

But growth requires relationships that see you as who you are becoming.

Forward-looking relationships:

- Challenge you in new ways

- Do not rely on your past accomplishments
- Hold you accountable to current standards
- Support long-term goals

These relationships may feel uncomfortable at first. That discomfort is often a sign of growth.

Connection as a Performance Multiplier

In sports, no one succeeds alone.

The same is true financially, professionally, and personally.

Connection improves:

- Decision-making
- Emotional regulation
- Long-term discipline
- Resilience during setbacks

Isolation magnifies mistakes. Community absorbs impact.

This is not about networking for advantage. It is about building a support system that keeps you grounded and progressing.

Choosing to Stay Connected on Purpose

Connection does not happen accidentally after sports.

You have to schedule it.

You have to prioritize it.

You have to protect it.

Just like training.

Former athletes who thrive long-term treat connection as part of their system, not a bonus. They invest in relationships with the same discipline they once invested in their sport.

Carrying the Team Mentality Forward

You may never wear the uniform again, but the team mindset still applies.

Show up prepared.

Do your job.

Support others.

Hold yourself accountable.

The arena changes. The principles remain.

Athlete Takeaways

- Loss of team connection is real and normal
- Isolation feels like independence but limits growth
- Mentorship replaces coaching after sports
- Honor the past without living in it
- Build new locker rooms that support who you are becoming

Staying connected does not mean staying stuck. It means carrying forward the parts of sports that made you better while allowing your identity, purpose, and community to evolve. That is how former athletes build lives that are not only successful, but connected, grounded, and resilient.

Disclaimers

This book is for educational purposes only.

The information provided in **Dance Money 101** is intended to help readers understand general financial concepts using dance-based analogies. It is not individualized financial, investment, tax, legal, or insurance advice.

Every financial situation is different. Your goals, income, career path, family circumstances, risk tolerance, and time horizon are unique. What works for one person may not be appropriate for another.

Not Financial, Investment, or Legal Advice

Nothing in this book should be interpreted as a recommendation to buy, sell, or hold any specific investment, financial product, or strategy.

This book does not replace advice from qualified professionals such as:

- Financial advisors
- Accountants or tax professionals
- Attorneys
- Insurance professionals

Before making financial decisions, readers should consult professionals who can evaluate their individual situation.

No Guarantees or Promises of Results

All investing involves risk, including the possible loss of principal.

Past performance does not guarantee future results. Markets fluctuate. Economic conditions change. Outcomes cannot be predicted or guaranteed.

The examples and scenarios in this book are illustrative only and may not reflect actual results or real-world outcomes.

Tax and Legal Information

Any discussion of taxes, retirement accounts, estate planning, or legal structures is general in nature.

Tax laws and regulations change frequently and vary by jurisdiction. Legal requirements differ based on location and personal circumstances.

Readers should seek personalized tax or legal advice before acting on any information related to these topics.

Performer and Career Considerations

This book discusses financial topics as they relate to dancers and former dancers, including freelance income, contract work, career transitions, and variable earnings.

It does not provide career placement services, employment advice, or guarantees related to income, compensation, or career success.

Use of Analogies

Dance and performing arts analogies are used to make financial concepts easier to understand.

These analogies are educational tools only and should not be interpreted literally. Financial decisions require analysis beyond analogy.

Personal Responsibility

By reading this book, you acknowledge that:

- You are responsible for your own financial decisions
- You understand that financial outcomes involve uncertainty
- You agree to seek appropriate professional guidance when needed

Education improves decision-making, but responsibility remains with the individual.

Contact Information

If you would like to learn more about the concepts discussed in this book or explore additional educational resources, **Pat Brown** can be found through public platforms including LinkedIn, Twitter, and via Google search.

For questions specifically related to **Dance Money 101**, you may contact Pat Brown at:

info@dancemoney101.com

Final Reminder

Financial success is built over time through discipline, planning, and consistency.

This book provides a framework, not a guarantee.

Use it as a guide, not a substitute for professional advice.

Glossary of Dance and Financial Terms

This glossary connects key financial concepts to familiar ideas from **dance**, making money easier to understand through the language, structure, and discipline performers already know.

Asset Allocation

Financial Definition:

How money is divided among different investment types such as stocks, bonds, and cash to balance risk and return.

Dance Comparison:

How effort, difficulty, and focus are distributed across training, rehearsal, performance, and recovery. Too much emphasis on one area without balance leads to instability and burnout.

Assets

Financial Definition:

Things you own that have value, such as cash, investments, real estate, or retirement accounts.

Dance Comparison:

Your strengths as a dancer. Technique, conditioning, versatility, experience, and preparation that contribute to long-term performance.

Bonds

Financial Definition:

Loans made to governments or companies that pay interest and return principal over time.

Dance Comparison:

Foundational technique and conditioning. Not flashy, but essential for control, consistency and stability under pressure.

Budget

Financial Definition:

A plan for how income is allocated toward expenses, savings, and goals.

Dance Comparison:

A rehearsal schedule or training plan. Without structure and timing, execution breaks down and progress stalls.

Cash Flow

Financial Definition:

Money coming in versus money going out.

Dance Comparison:

Energy management. If you expend too much early without recovery, performance suffers later.

Compounding

Financial Definition:

Earnings that generate additional earnings over time.

Dance Comparison:

Daily practice and muscle memory. Small, consistent improvements build momentum and long-term mastery.

Credit

Financial Definition:

The ability to borrow money with the promise of repayment.

Dance Comparison:

Trust and reputation. When managed well, it creates opportunities. When abused, it limits future options.

Debt

Financial Definition:

Money borrowed that must be repaid, often with interest.

Dance Comparison:

Extra weight or strain. Manageable in small amounts, but damaging when excessive or ignored.

Diversification

Financial Definition:

Spreading investments across different assets to reduce risk.

Dance Comparison:

Not relying on one role, one company, or one income source to sustain your entire career.

Emergency Fund

Financial Definition:

Savings set aside for unexpected expenses.

Dance Comparison:

Injury prevention and recovery resources. You hope you never need them, but they keep your career from collapsing when something goes wrong.

ETF (Exchange-Traded Fund)

Financial Definition:

A fund that holds many investments and trades like a stock.

Dance Comparison:

An ensemble piece. Stronger and more stable than performing alone.

Fees / Expense Ratios

Financial Definition:

Costs associated with managing investments.

Dance Comparison:

Small technical mistakes. Individually minor, but over time they quietly drain performance and progress.

Growth Investing

Financial Definition:

Investing in companies expected to grow faster than average.

Dance Comparison:

High-difficulty choreography. Greater upside, but only works when fundamentals are solid.

Insurance

Financial Definition:

Protection against financial loss from unexpected events.

Dance Comparison:

Physical therapy, conditioning, and safety protocols. You don't perform without protection when risk increases.

Liquidity

Financial Definition:

How easily money can be accessed without penalty or delay.

Dance Comparison:

Flexibility in scheduling and contracts. The ability to adjust quickly when opportunities or setbacks arise.

Net Worth

Financial Definition:

Assets minus liabilities.

Dance Comparison:

Your overall career position. Not one performance, but the cumulative result of choices over time.

Rebalancing

Financial Definition:

Adjusting investments back to their intended mix over time.

Dance Comparison:

Career and training adjustments. Refining focus to restore balance and sustainability.

Risk

Financial Definition:

The chance that outcomes differ from expectations, including loss.

Dance Comparison:

Difficulty selection. Higher difficulty increases potential reward but also increases the chance of mistakes.

Roth IRA

Financial Definition:

A retirement account where money grows tax-free if rules are followed.

Dance Comparison:

Early discipline that creates a cleaner finish later in your career.

Stocks

Financial Definition:

Ownership shares in a company.

Dance Comparison:

Lead roles. High impact and growth potential, but they need support and balance to succeed.

Tax-Advantaged Accounts

Financial Definition:

Accounts that provide tax benefits, often with rules and restrictions.

Dance Comparison:

Structured training programs. The rules exist to improve long-term outcomes.

Volatility

Financial Definition:

Short-term ups and downs in market value.

Dance Comparison:

A wobble during a routine. Normal unless you panic and lose control.

Permanent Loss

Financial Definition:

Money that cannot recover due to poor decisions or panic.

Dance Comparison:

A fall caused by abandoning fundamentals.

Total Return

Financial Definition:

Investment return from both price growth and income.

Dance Comparison:

The full performance evaluation. Every element matters, not just one moment.

Value Investing

Financial Definition:

Investing in assets believed to be undervalued.

Dance Comparison:

Clean execution over flash. Less showy, more consistent results.

Yield

Financial Definition:

Income generated from an investment.

Dance Comparison:

Reliable performance work. Not glamorous, but steady and dependable.

Final Note

This glossary reinforces one core principle:

Financial success, like success in **dance**, comes from balance, discipline, timing, and repetition.

That philosophy runs through ***Dance Money 101*** and continues long after the final performance.

Pat Brown OLB, University of Kansas

Made in the USA
Monee, IL
04 November 2026

67387584R00128